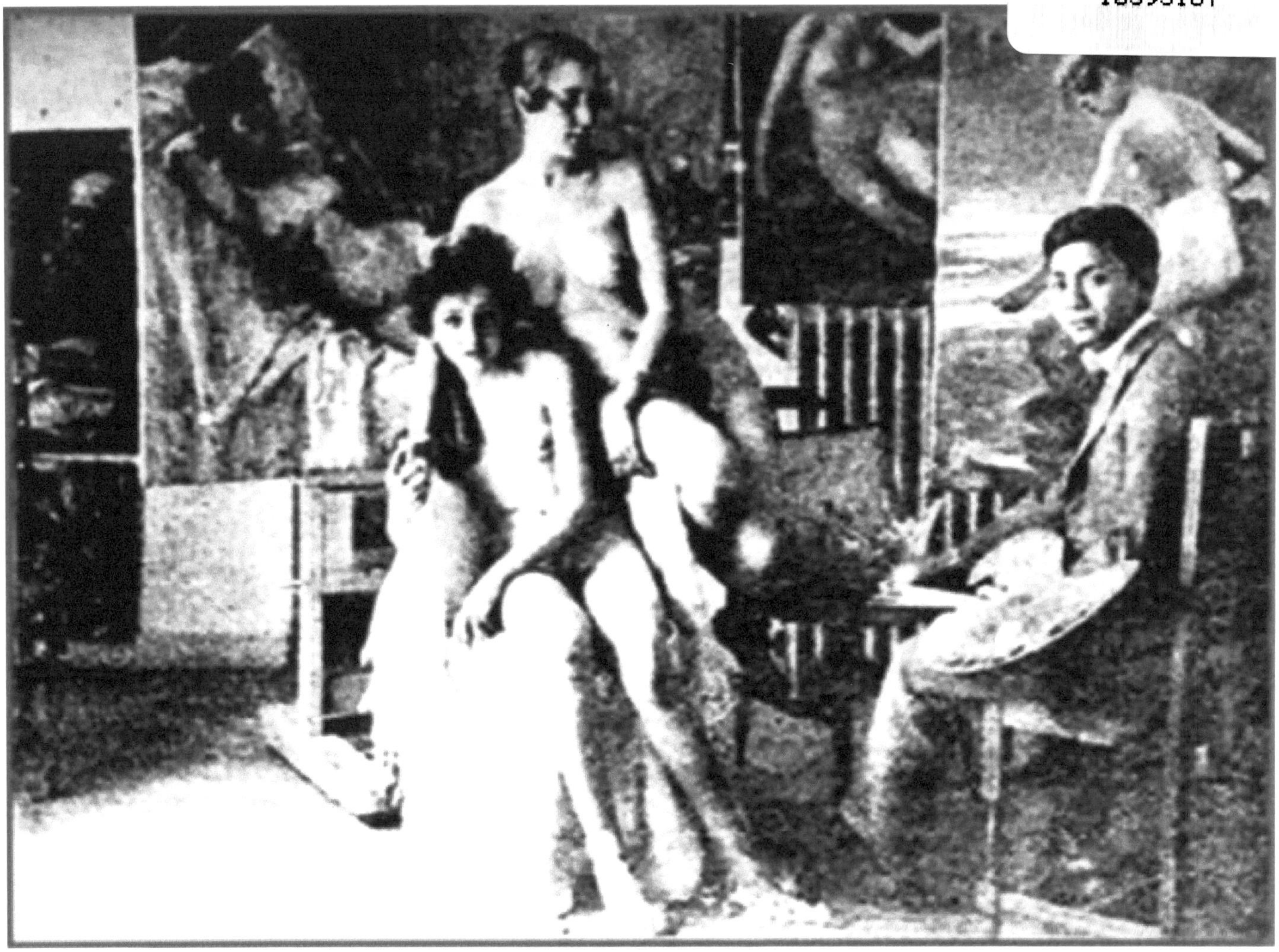

I0393167

Fernando Cueto Amorsolo posing for a posterity picture holding a painter's palette, along with 2 of her nude Caucasian models (simoun image @google, from Phils My Phils at facebook.)

WELCOME! We hope you enjoy this Fave Art-11 album collection of Pinoy Nude Art. Most art works are copied from the internet, posters, pictures and books. Most are collector's items and can be seen in famous galleries and private homes. The originals are very expensive but copies are available from some dealers. You may display this book as coffee table book in your living room, as conversation piece. You may give this as gift. You may cut out and frame each page. Each art work is 8.5x11 inches and suitable for framing, and for wall decors.

The ISBN Code Numbers of this book are:
ISBN-13: 978- 1544219554 & ISBN-10: 1544219555
Printed in USA. Free to copy by anybody. Why copy? Just buy the book.
My other books list can be accessed at:
http://tinyurl.com/mj76ccq and http://www.jobelizes6.wix.com/mysite.
My contact email is job_elizes@yahoo.com. (Tatay Jobo Elizes, Pub.)

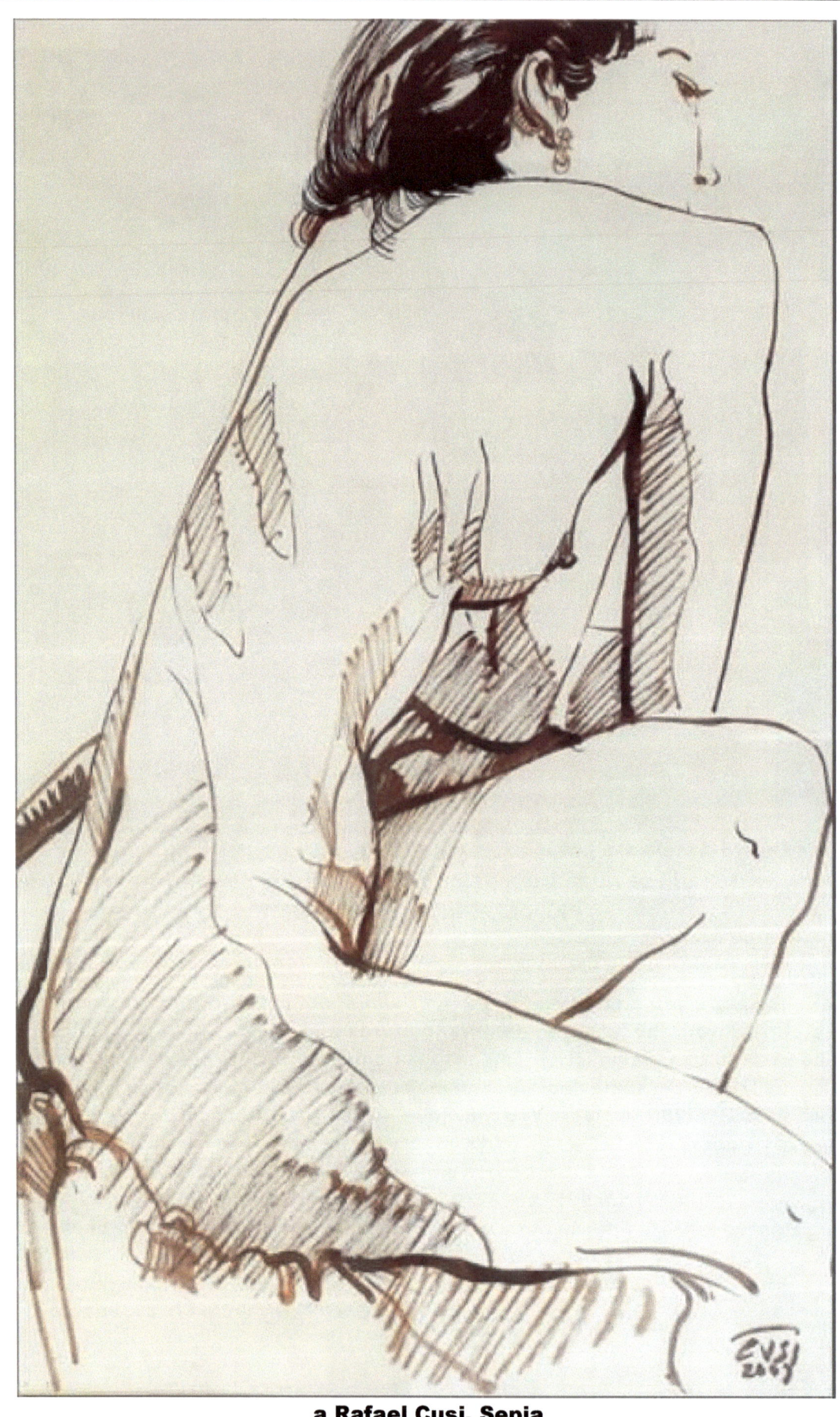

a Rafael Cusi, Sepia

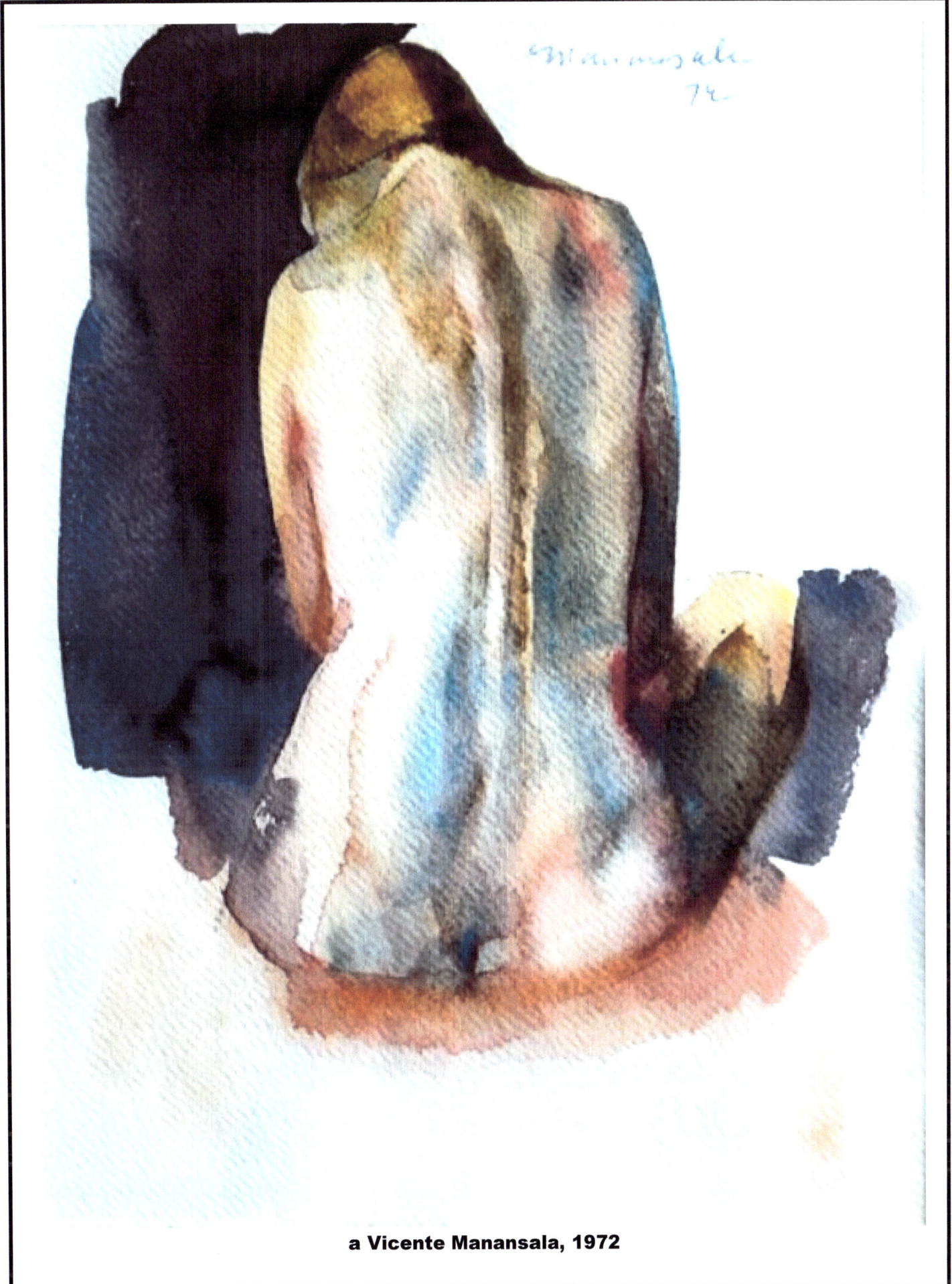

a Vicente Manansala, 1972

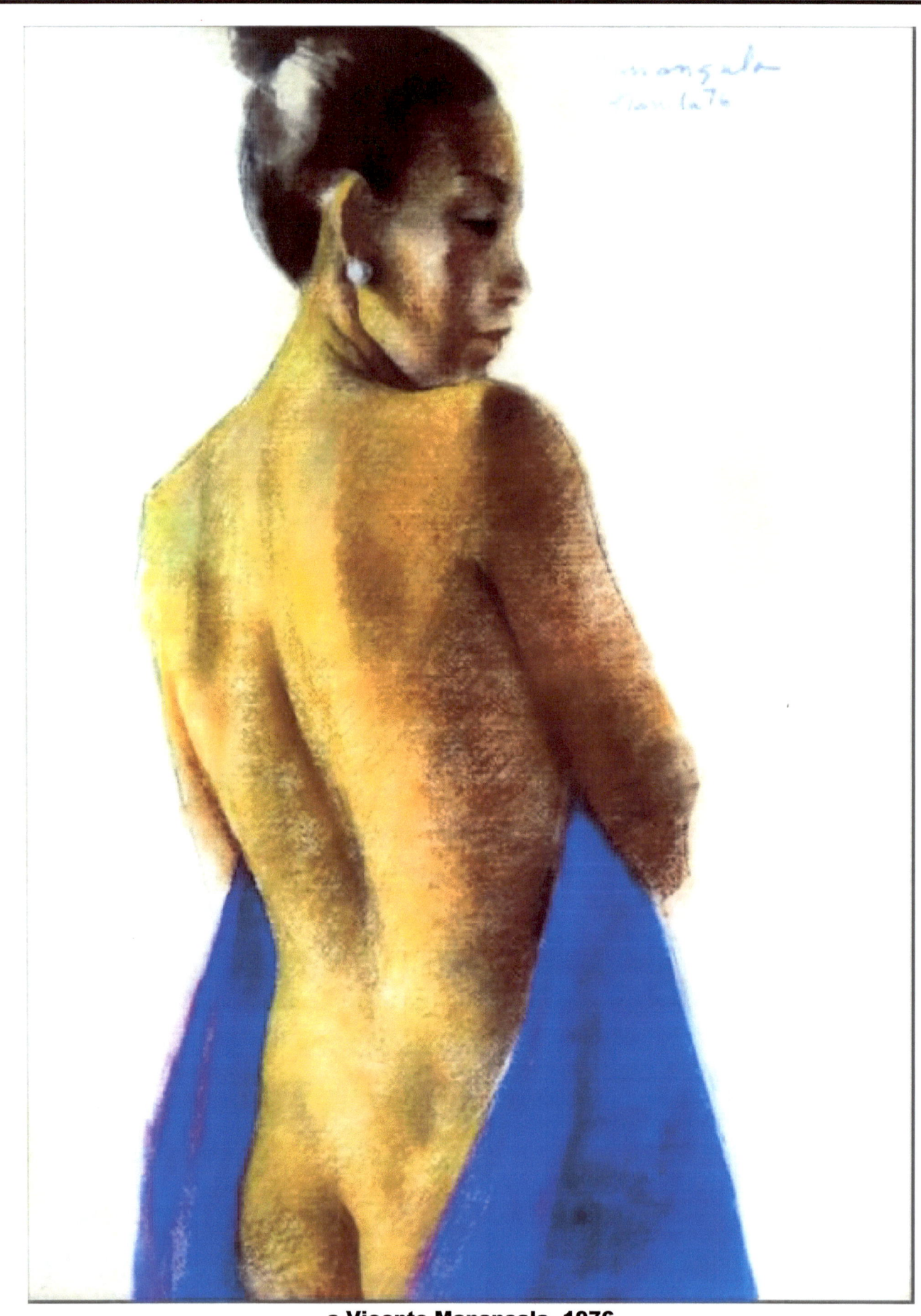

a Vicente Manansala, 1976

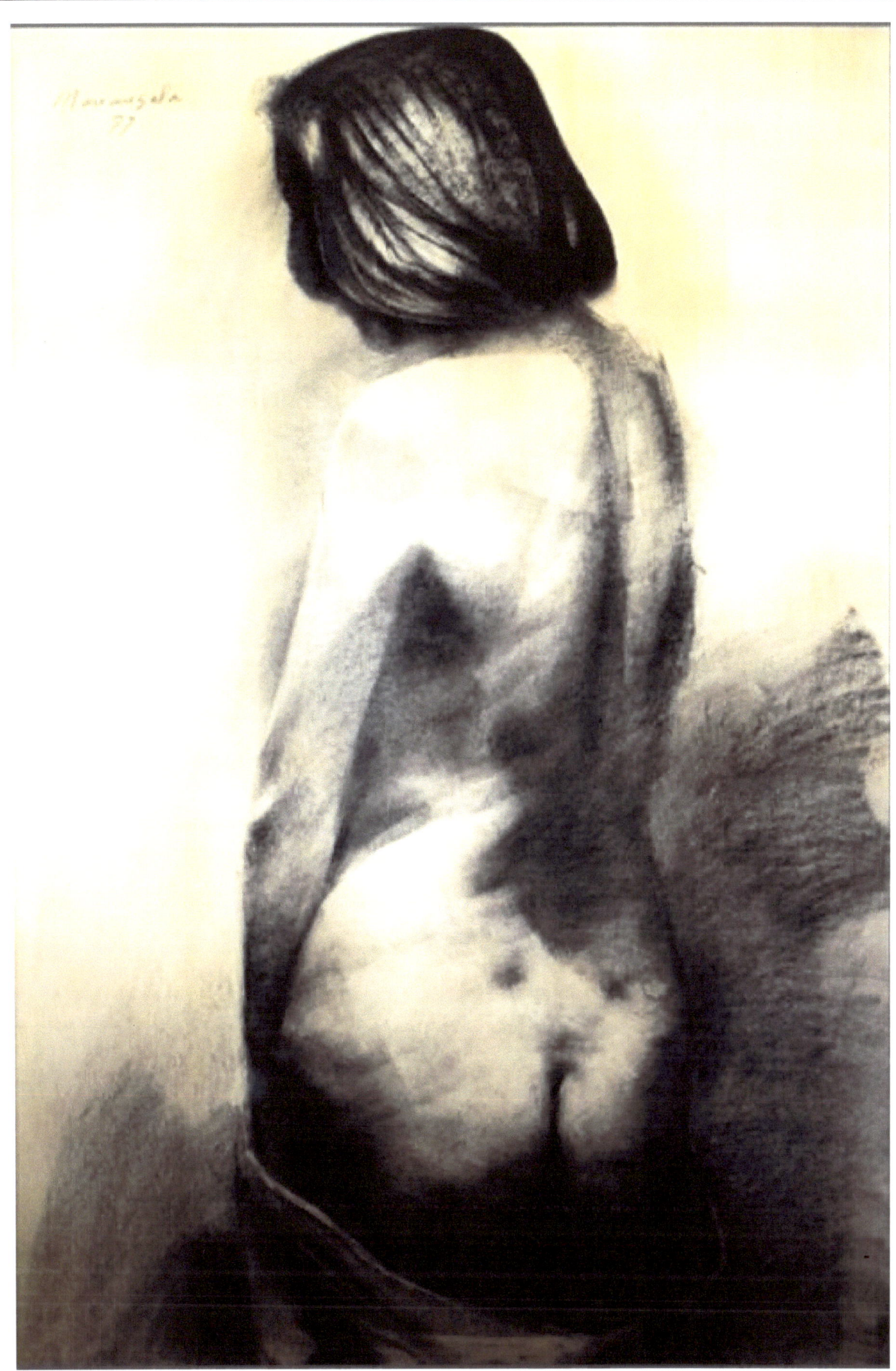

a Vicente Manansala, 1976

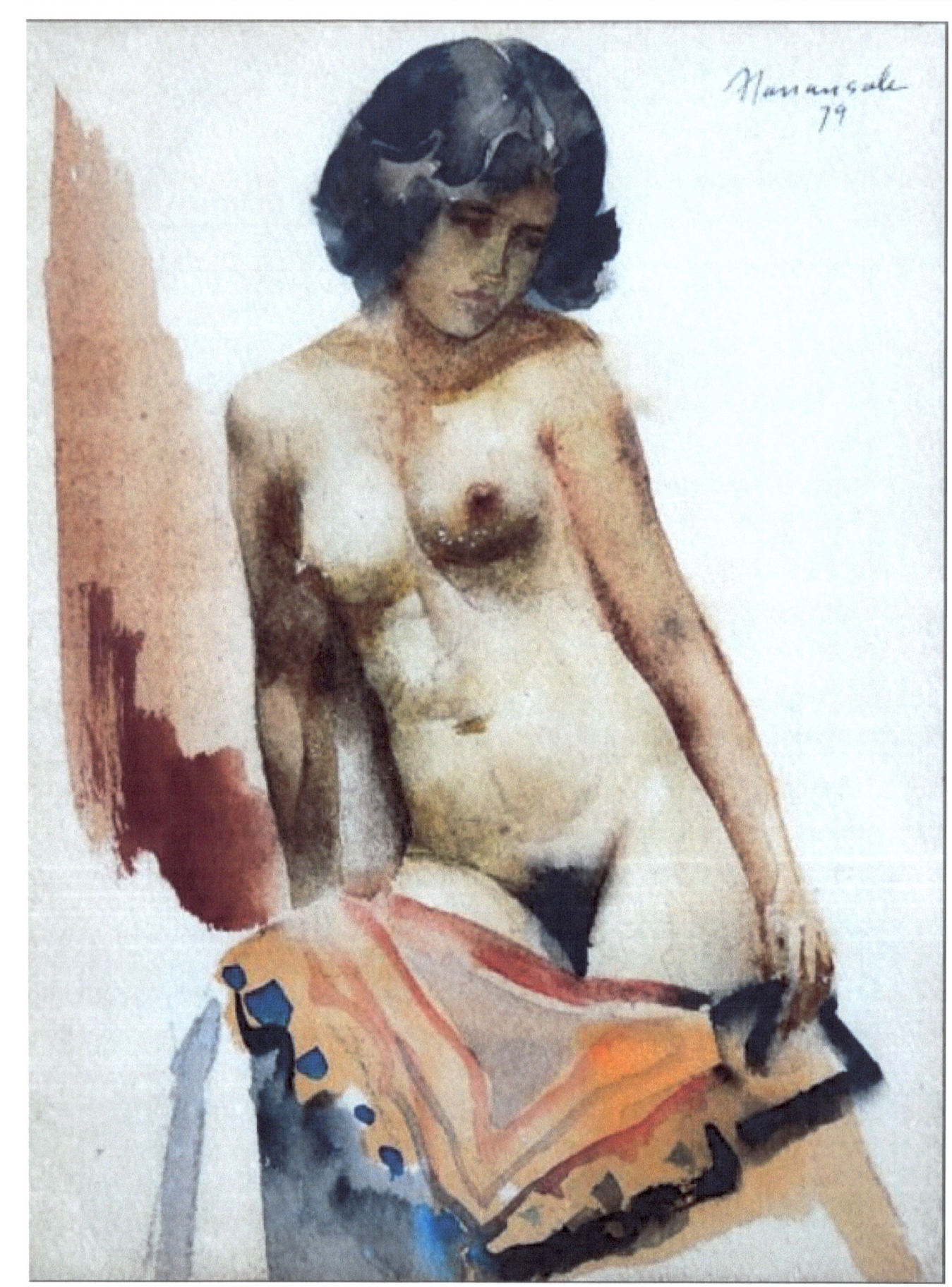

a Vicente Manansala, 1979

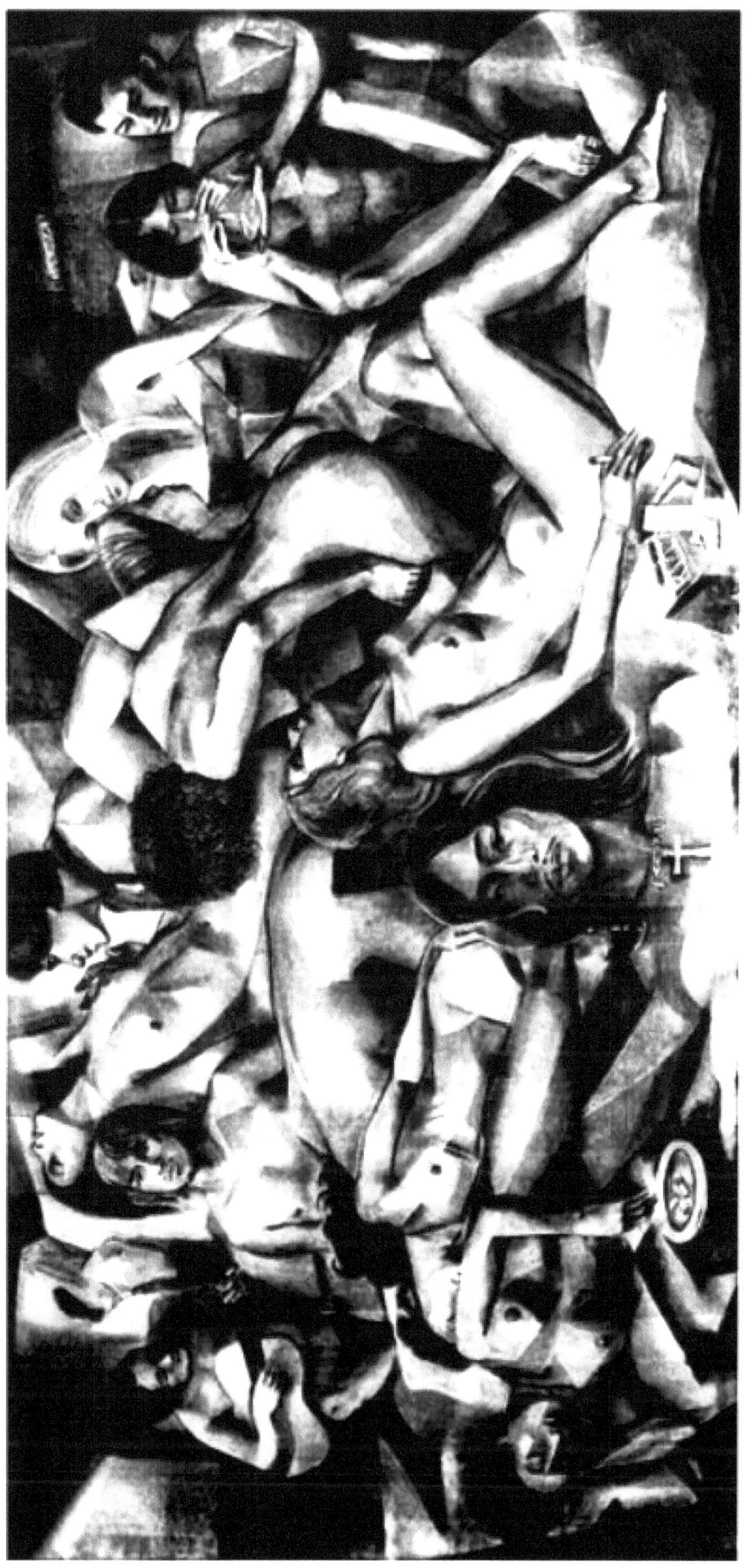

a Vicente Manansala, 1974, London

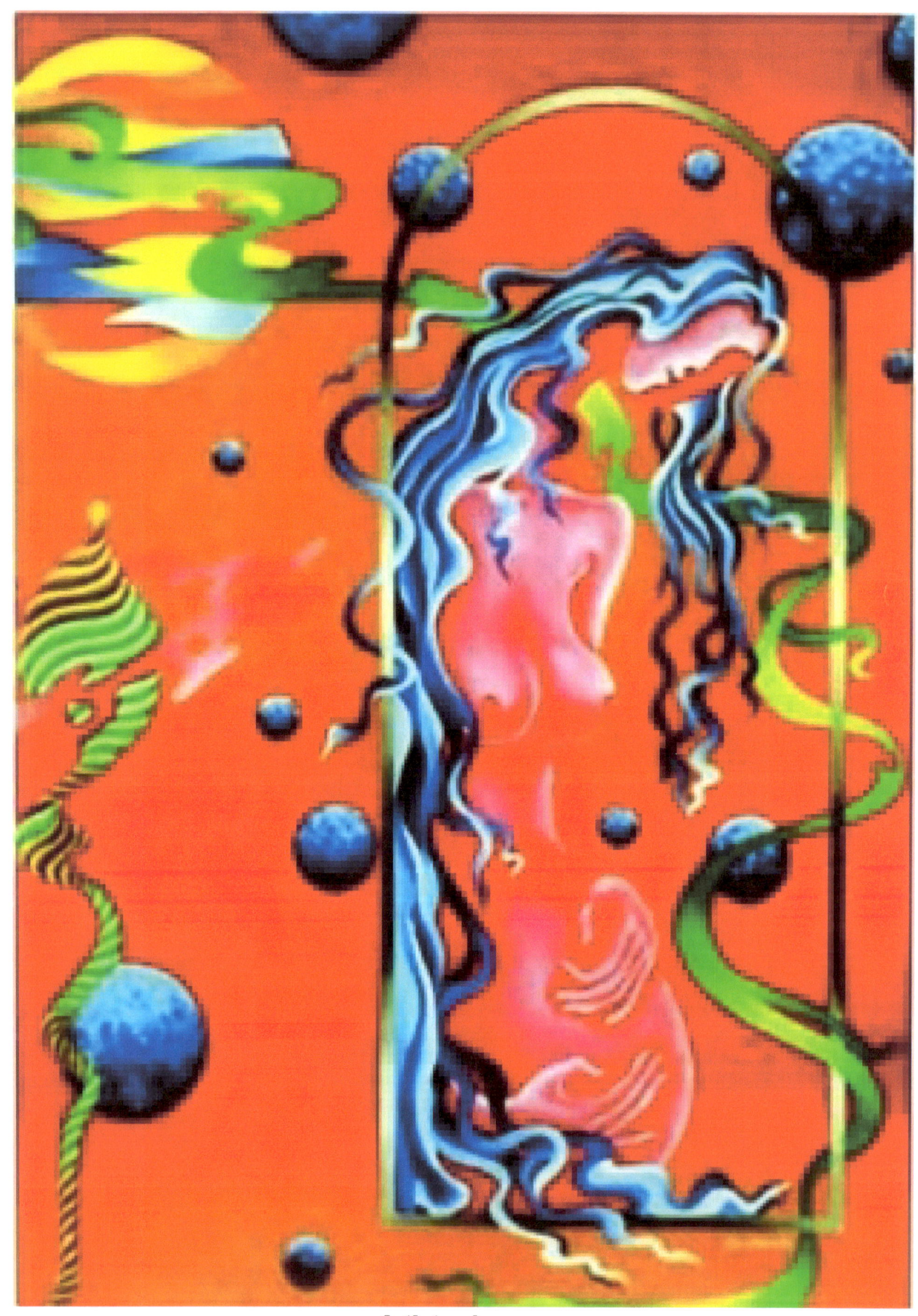

Artist unknown

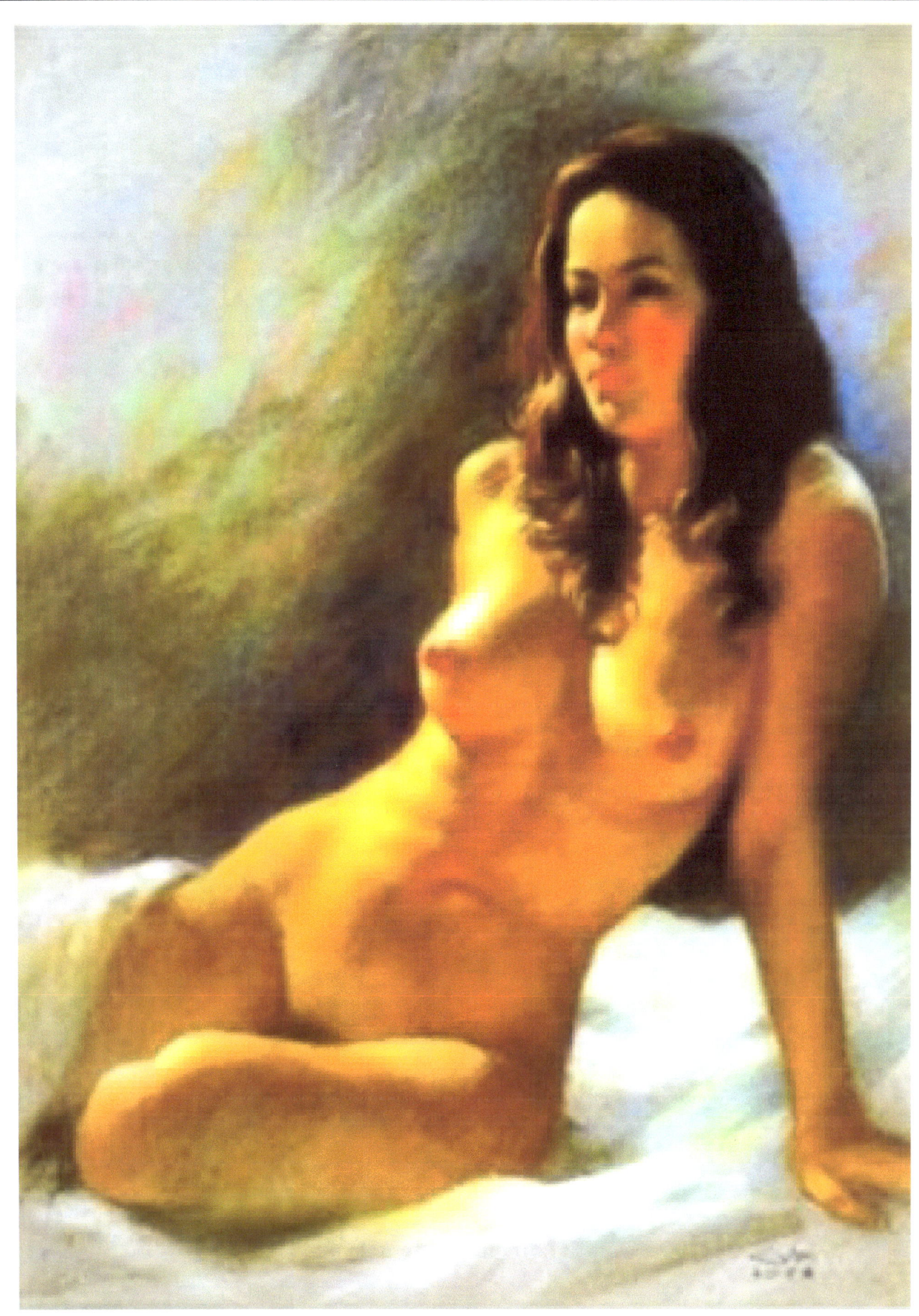

Artist unknown

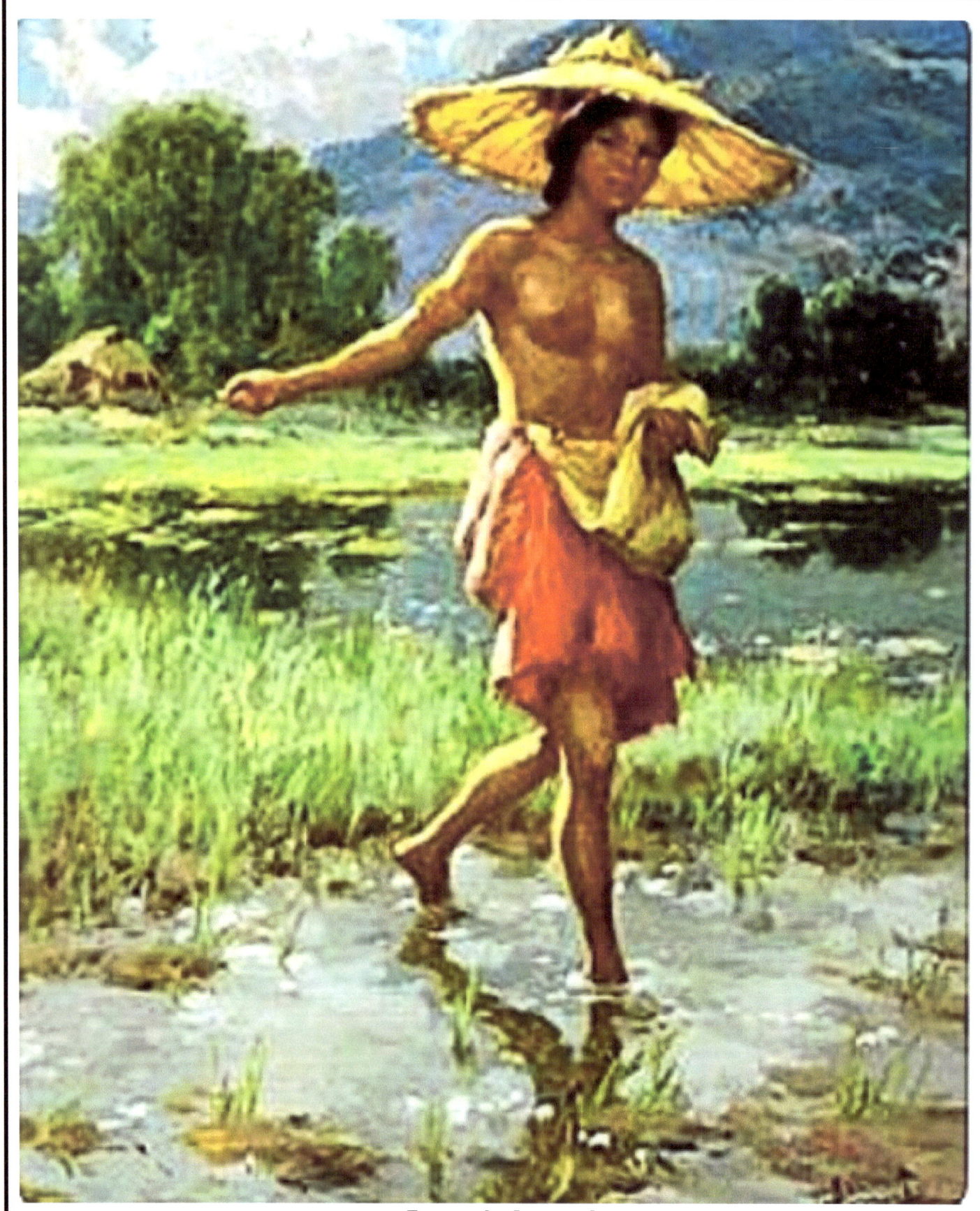

a Fernando Amorsolo

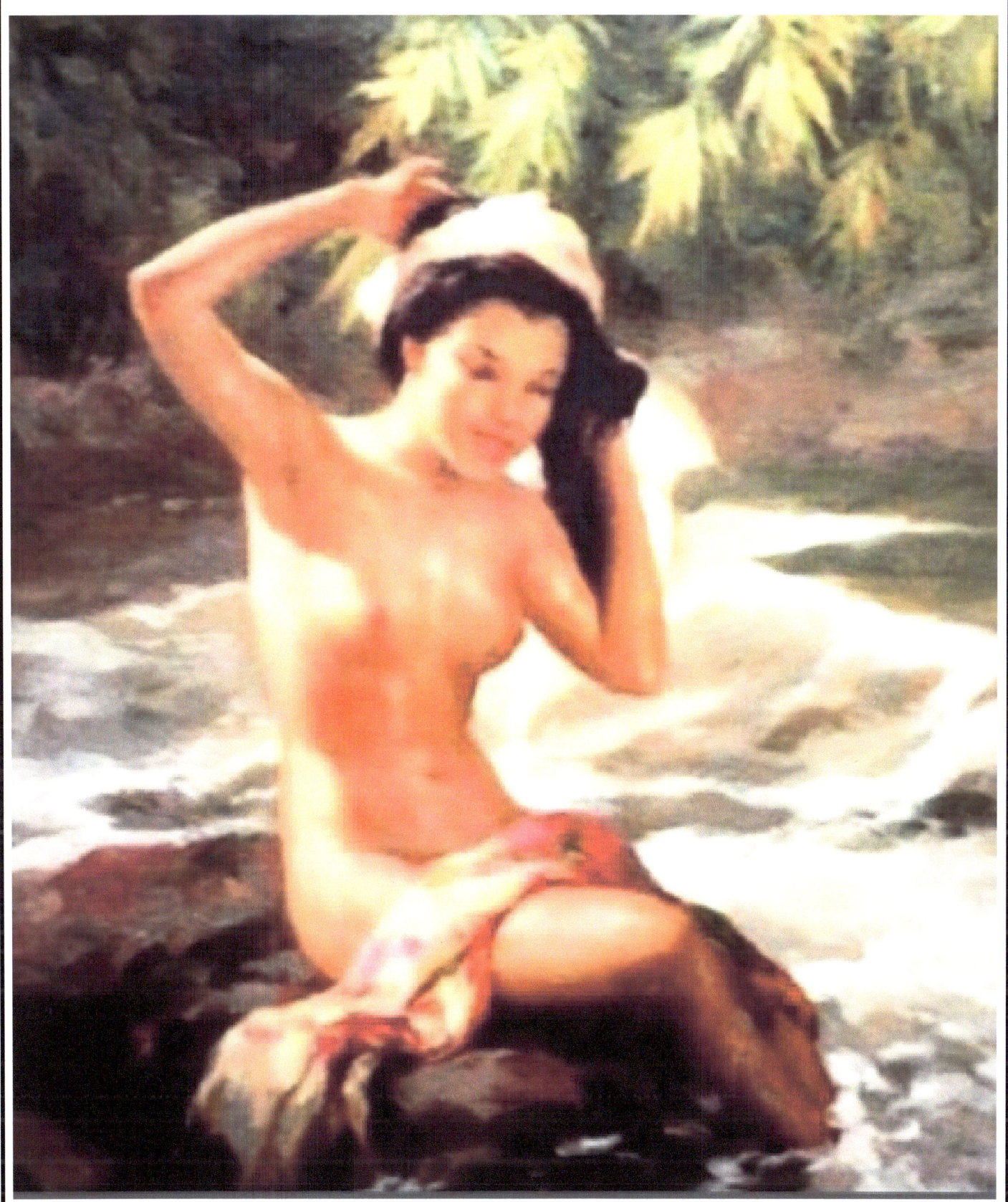

a Fernando Amorsolo

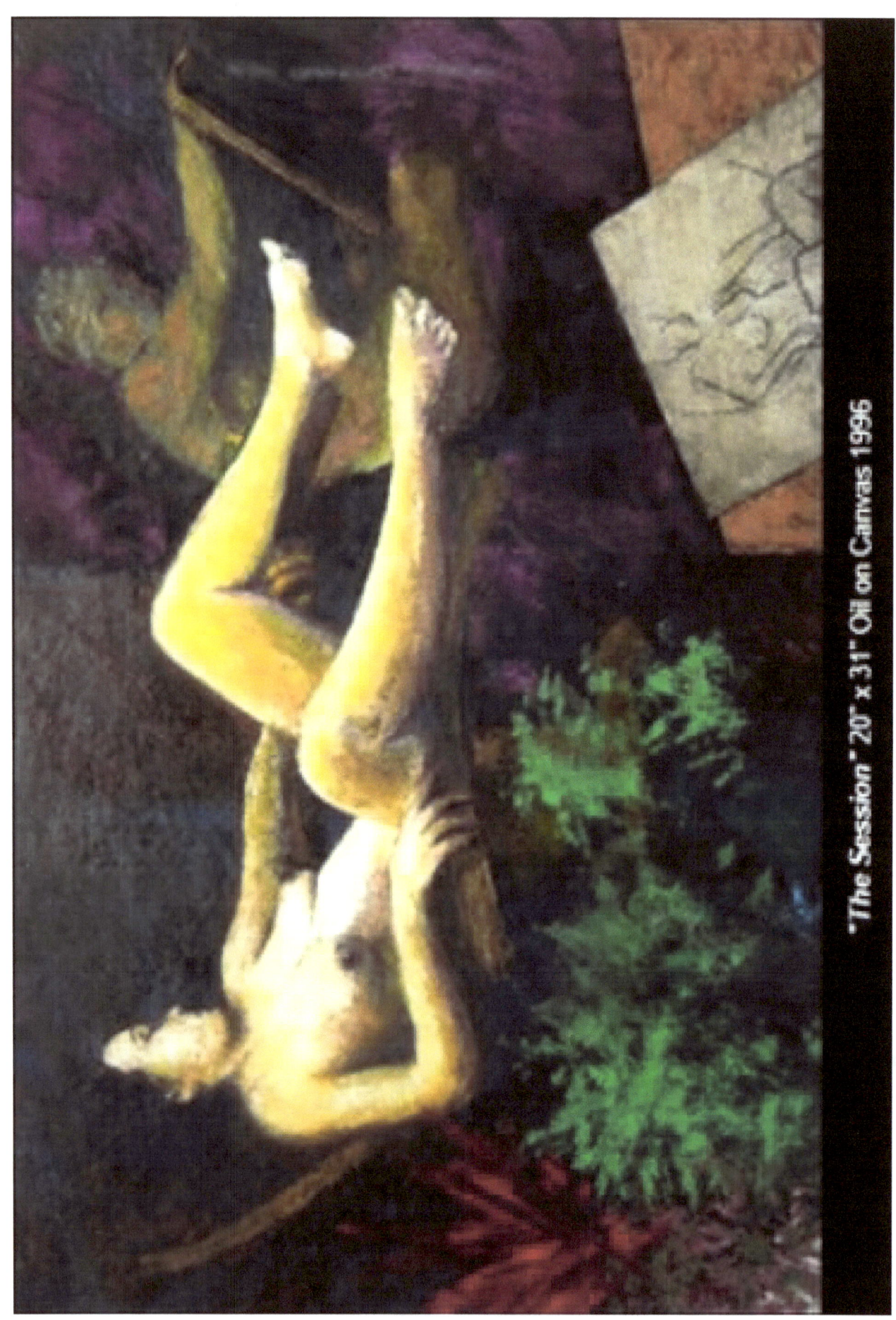

"The Session" 20" x 31" Oil on Canvas 1996

an Elizalde Navarro

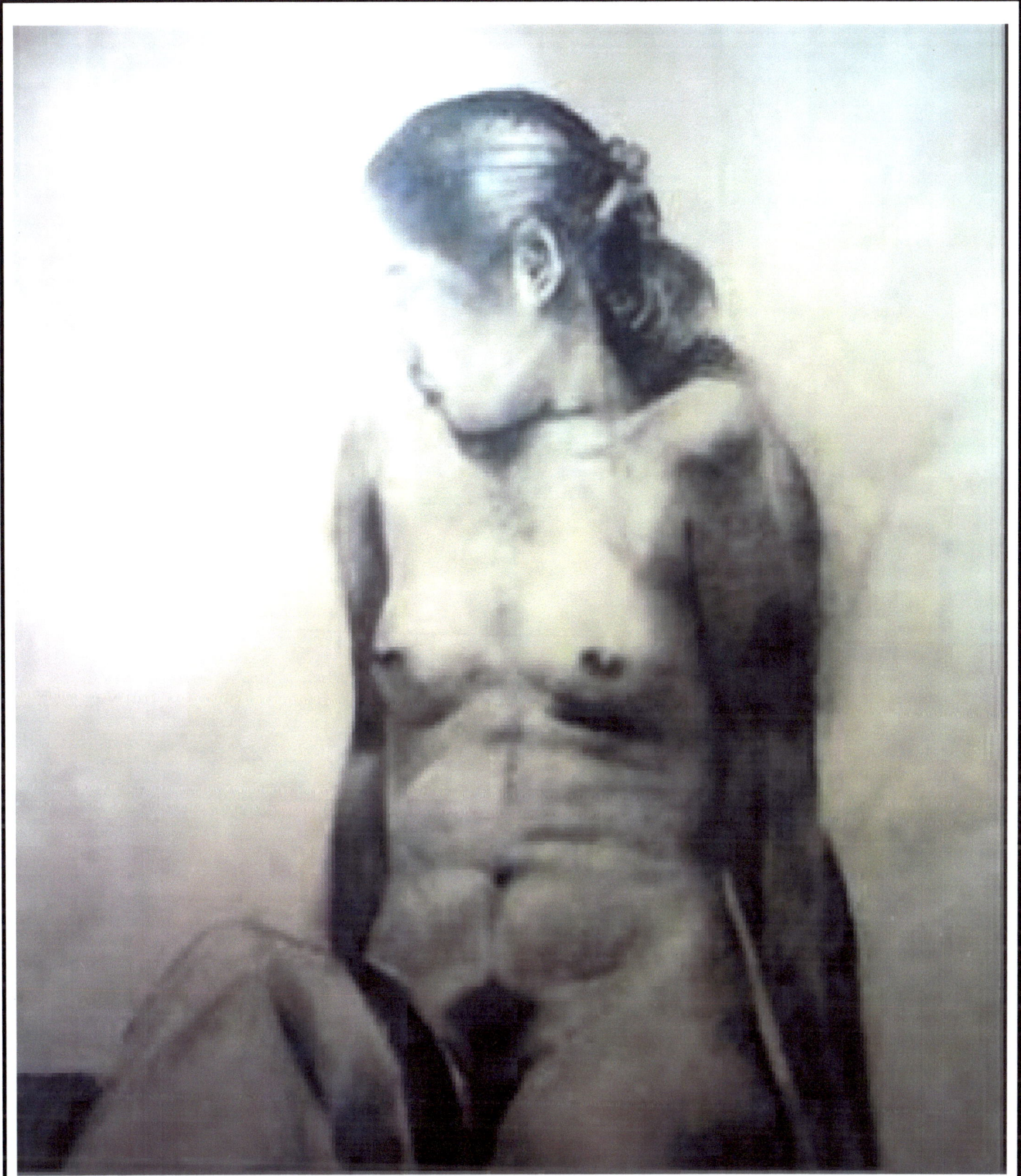

Artist unknown

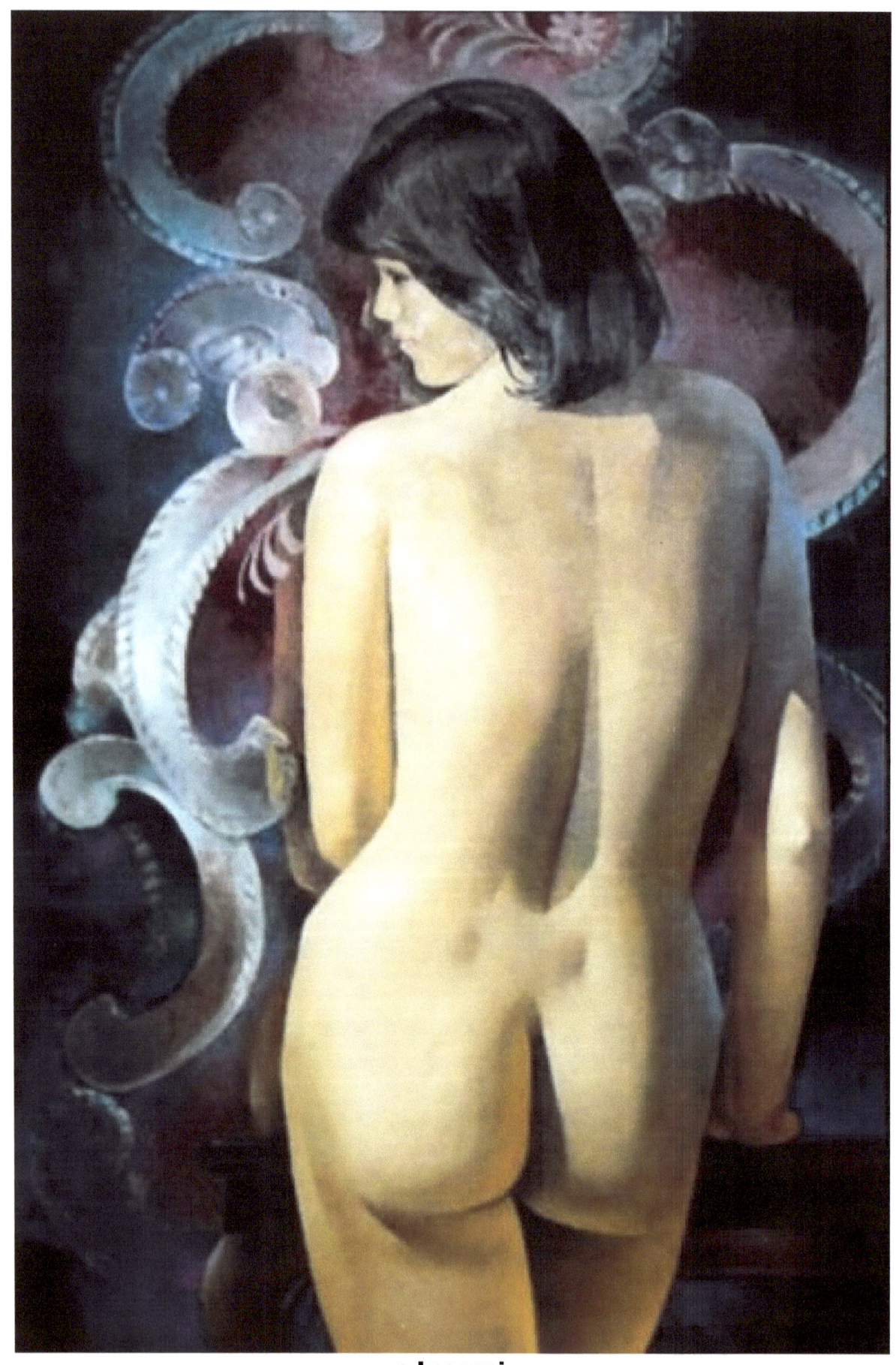

a Legaspi

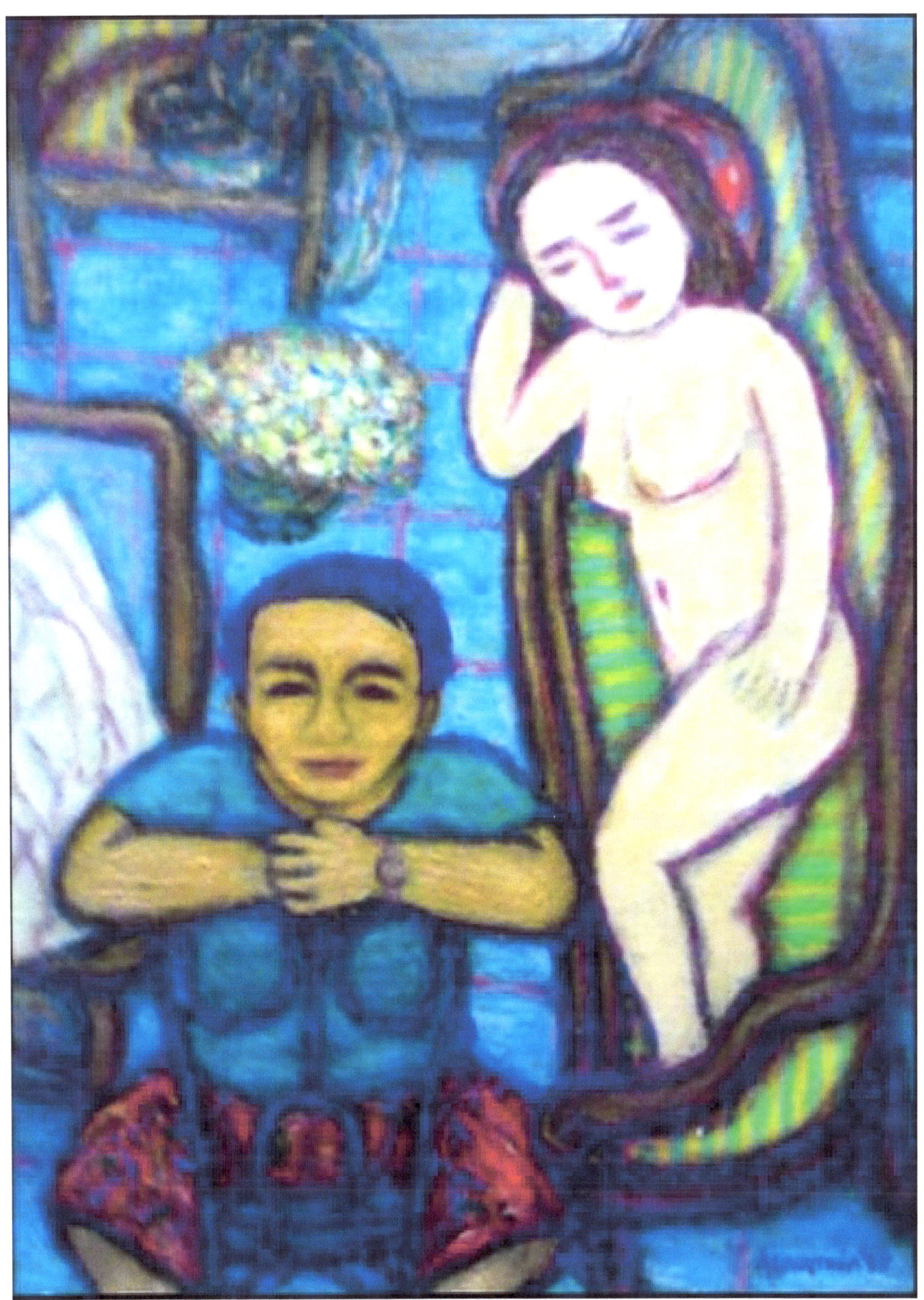

an Antonio Austria

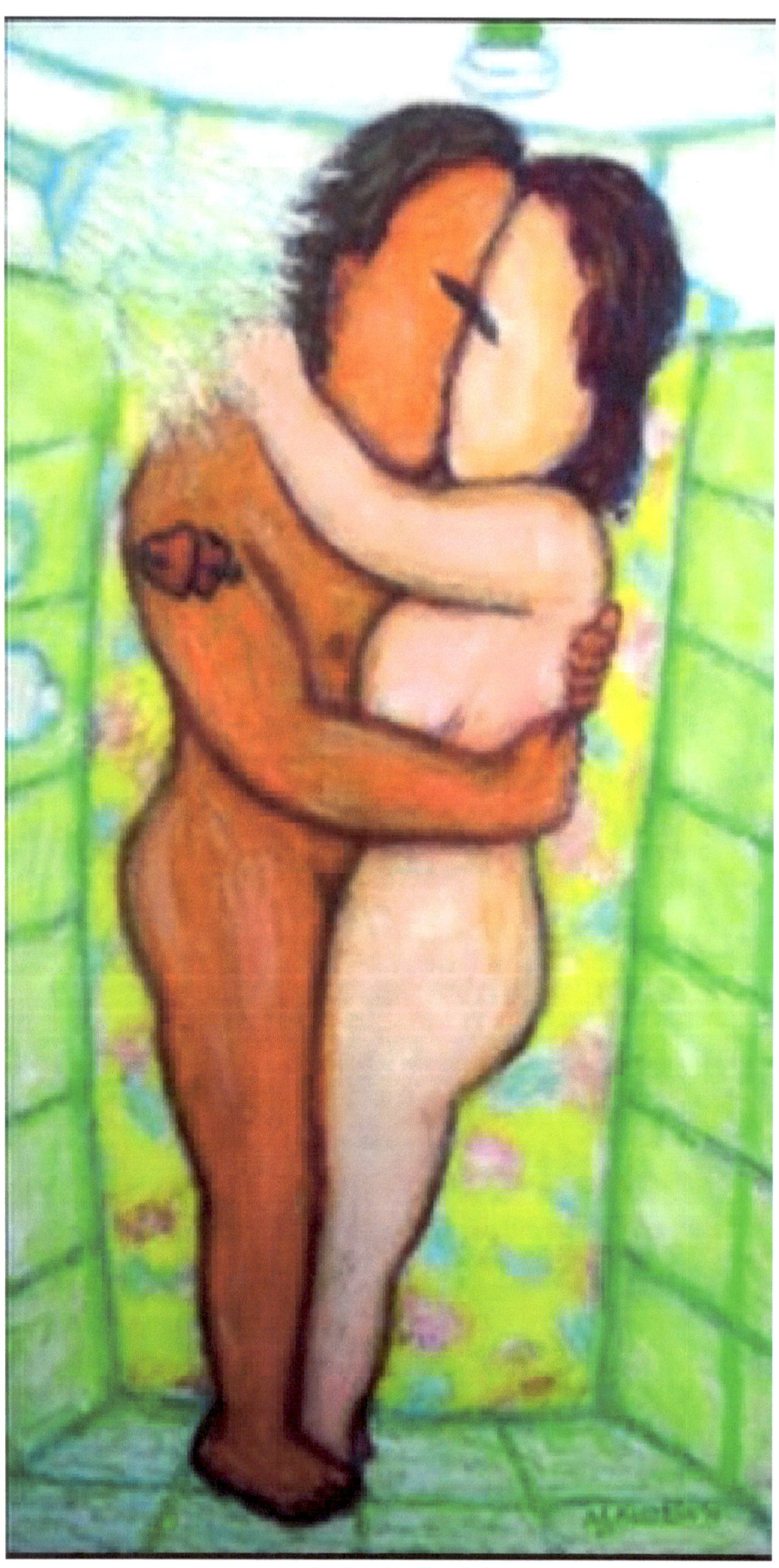

an Antonio Austria

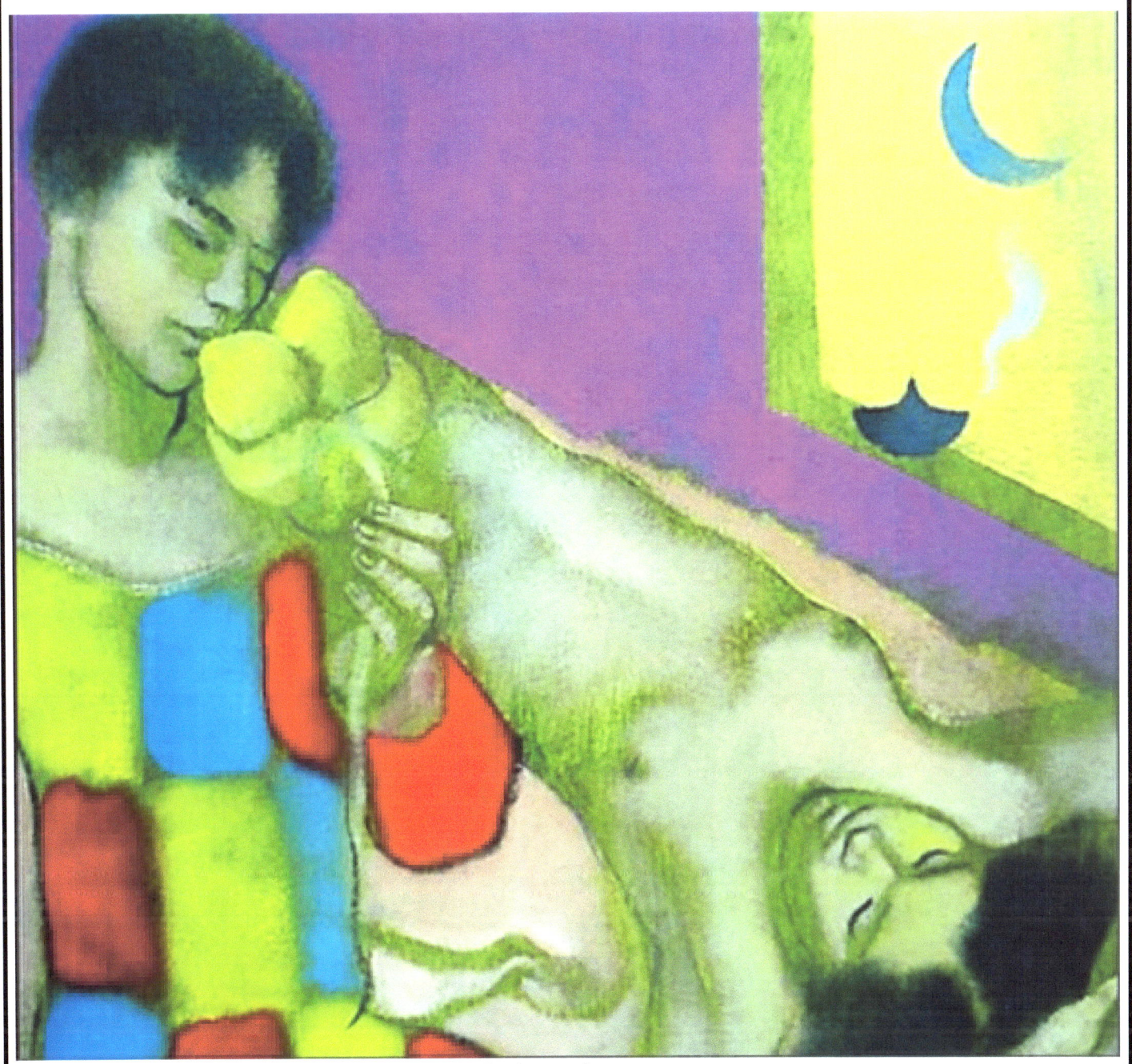

Artist unknown

WELCOME! We hope you enjoy this Fave Art-11 album collection of Pinoy Nude Art. Most art works are copied from the internet, posters, pictures and books. Most are collector's items and can be seen in famous galleries and private homes. The originals are very expensive but copies are available from some dealers. You may display this book as coffee table book in your living room, as conversation piece. You may give this as gift. You may cut out and frame each page. Each art work is 8.5x11 inches and suitable for framing, and for wall decors.

The ISBN Code Numbers of this book are:
ISBN-13: 978- 1544219554 & ISBN-10: 1544219555
Printed in USA. Free to copy by anybody. Why copy? Just buy the book.
My other books list can be accessed at:
http://tinyurl.com/mj76ccq and http://www.jobelizes6.wix.com/mysite.
My contact email is job_elizes@yahoo.com. (Tatay Jobo Elizes, Pub.)

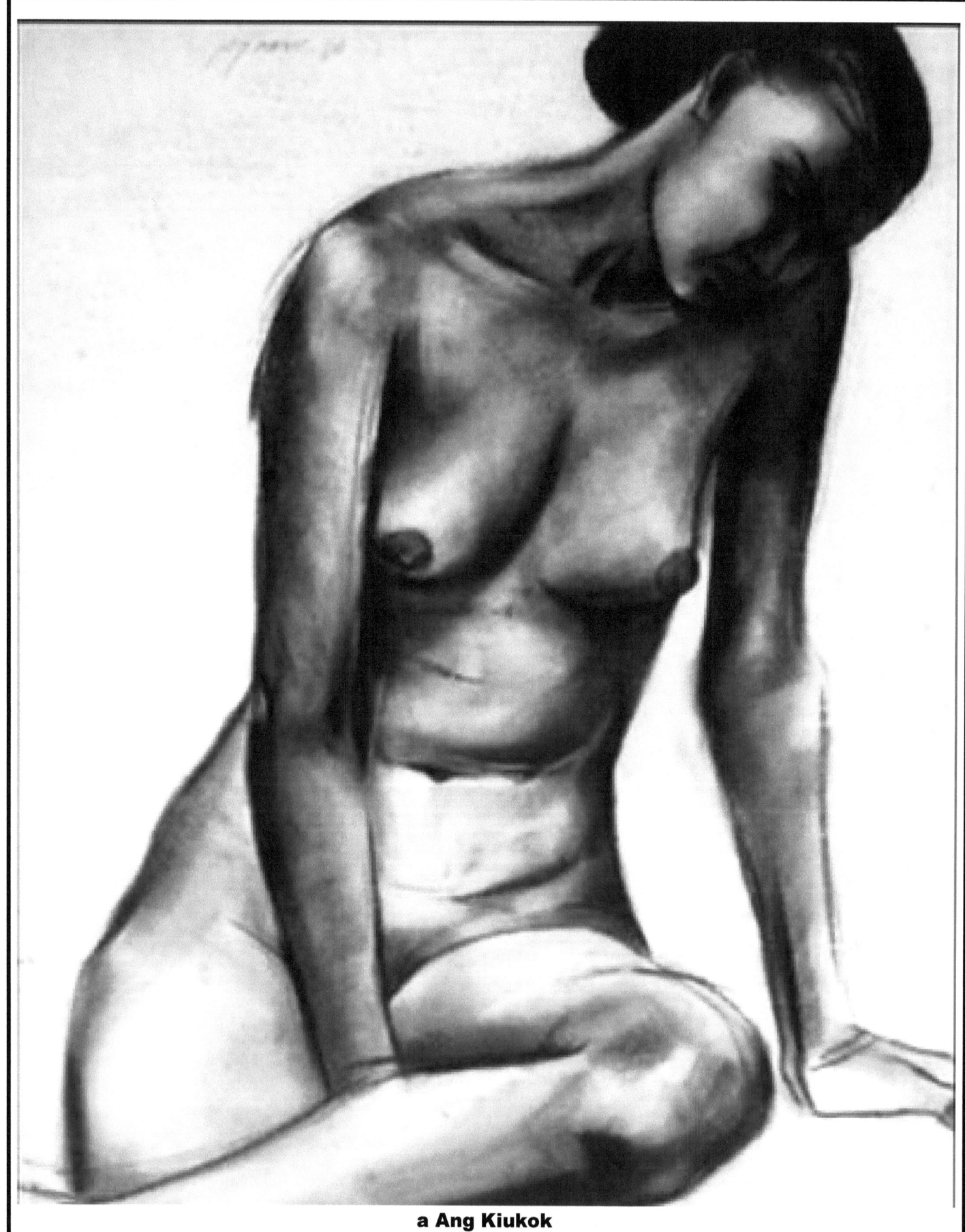

a Ang Kiukok

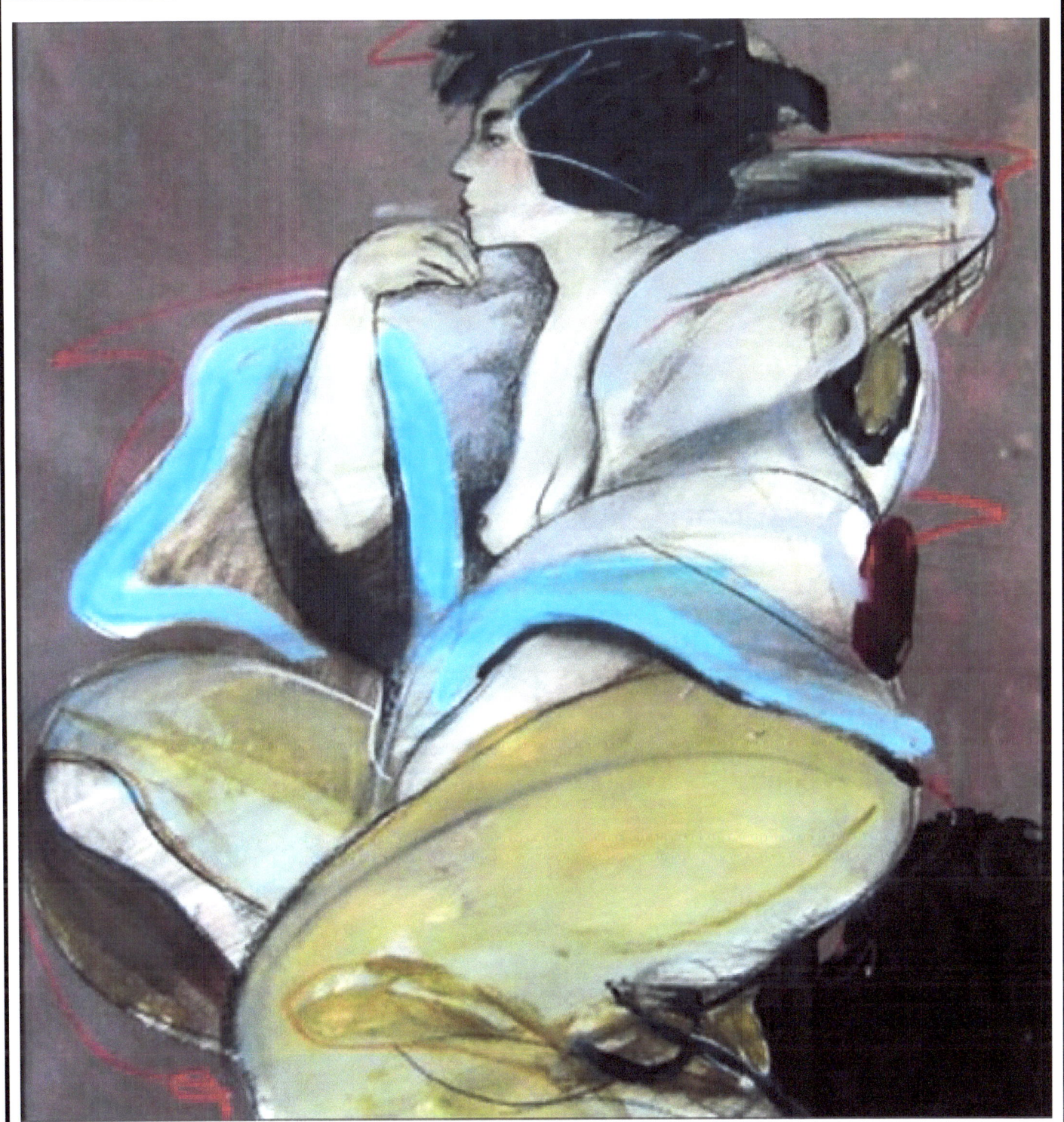

a Ang Liukok

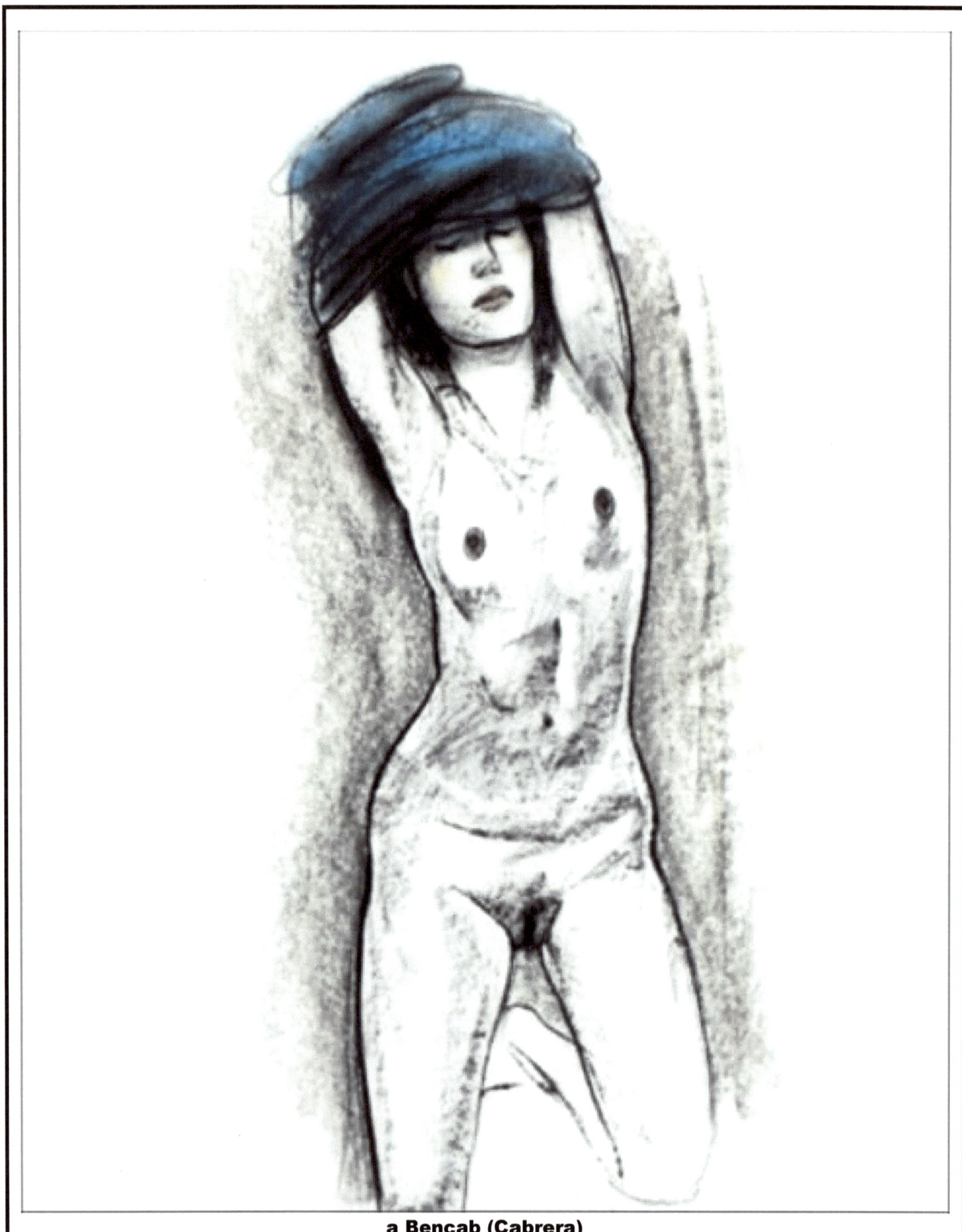

a Bencab (Cabrera)

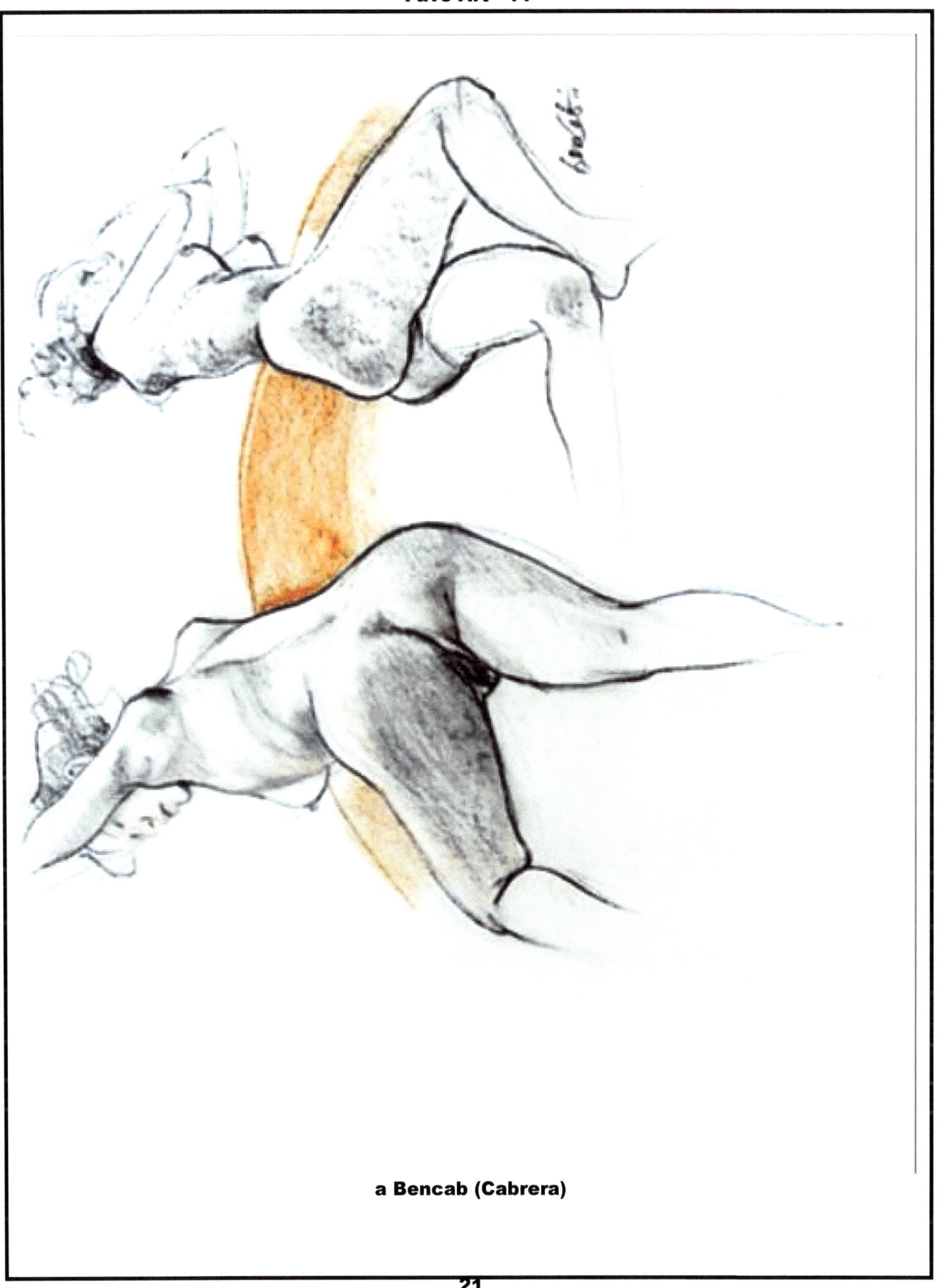

a Bencab (Cabrera)

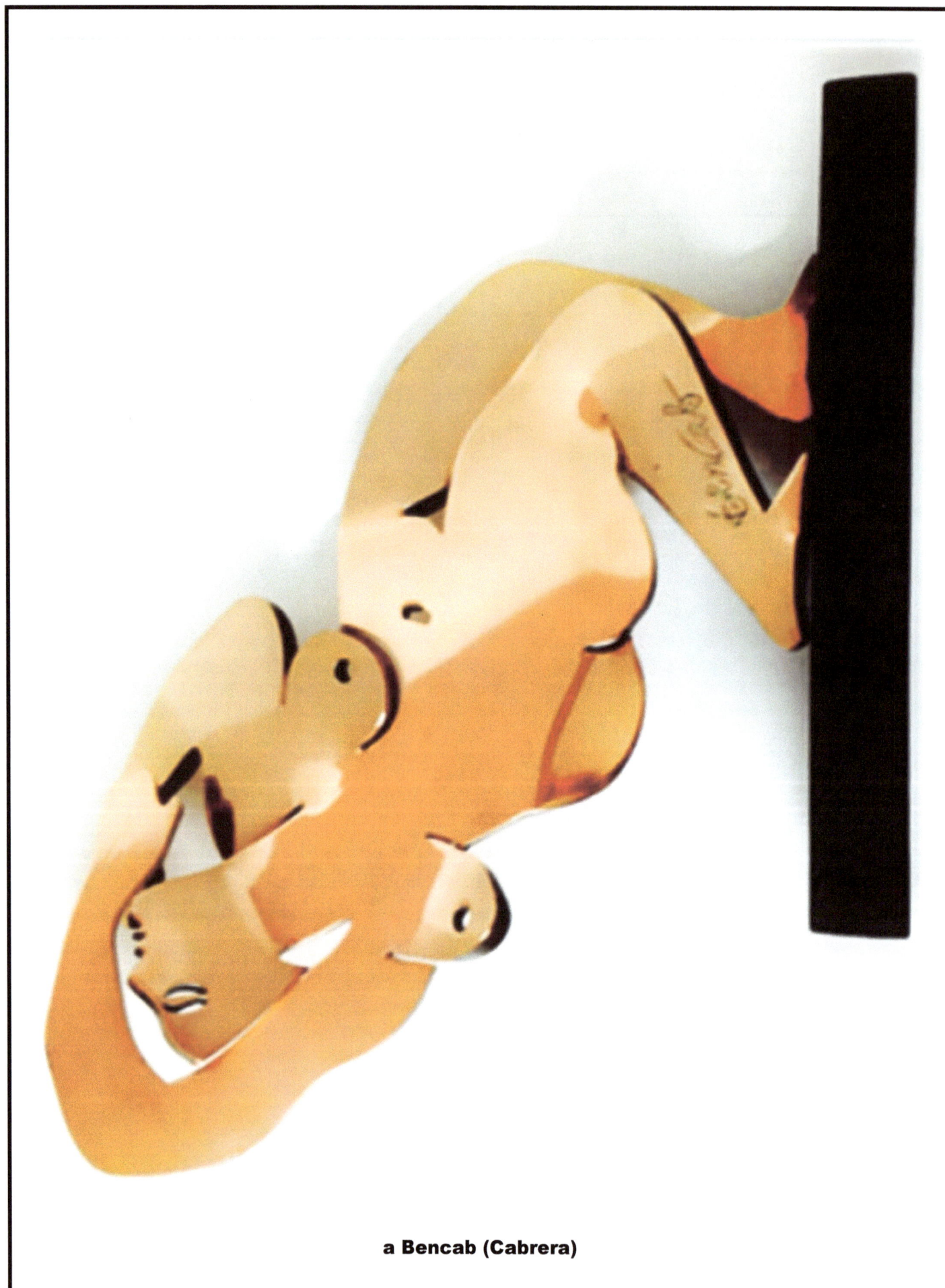

a Bencab (Cabrera)

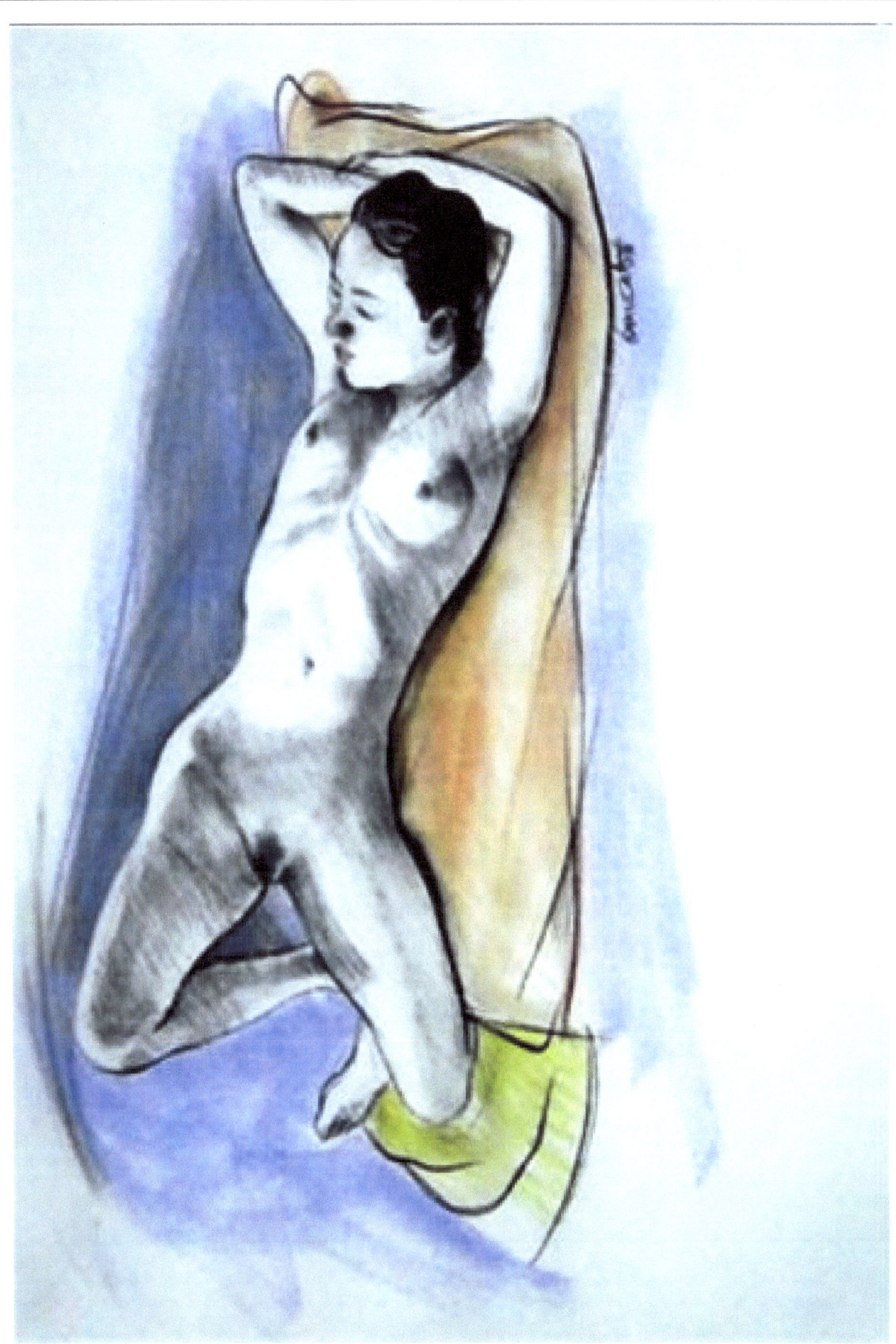

a Bencab (Cabrera)

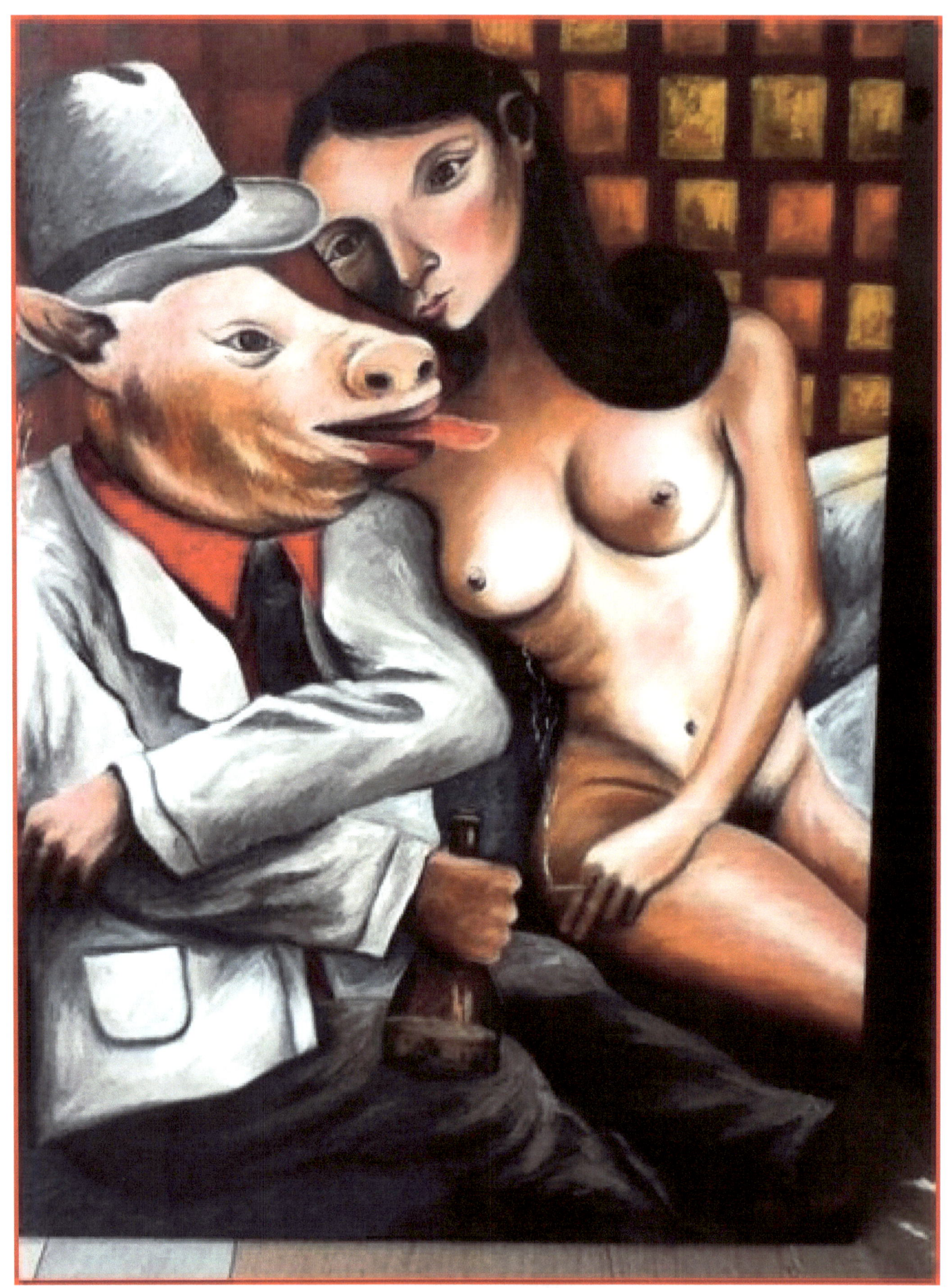

a Hermes Alegre

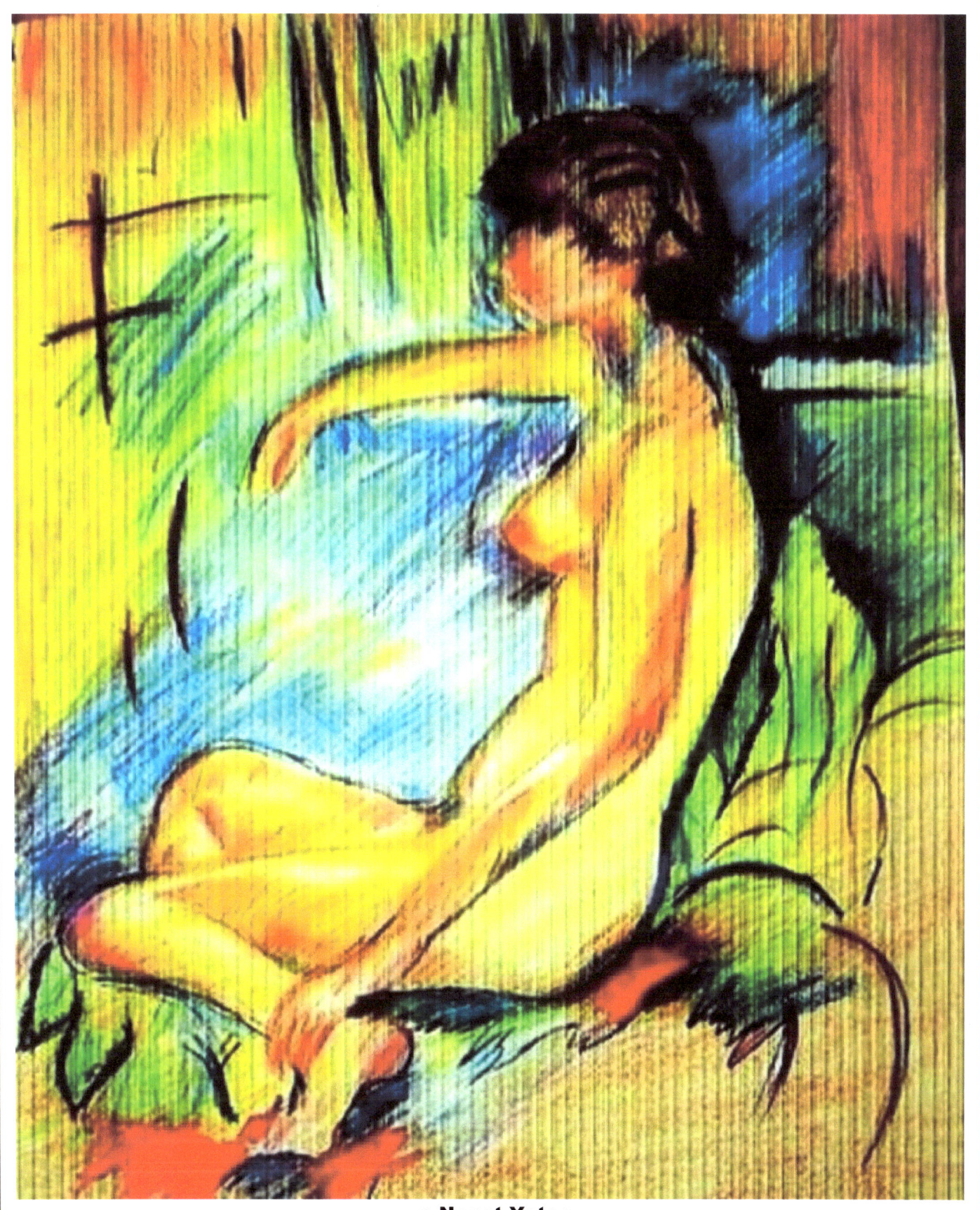

a Nanet Yatco

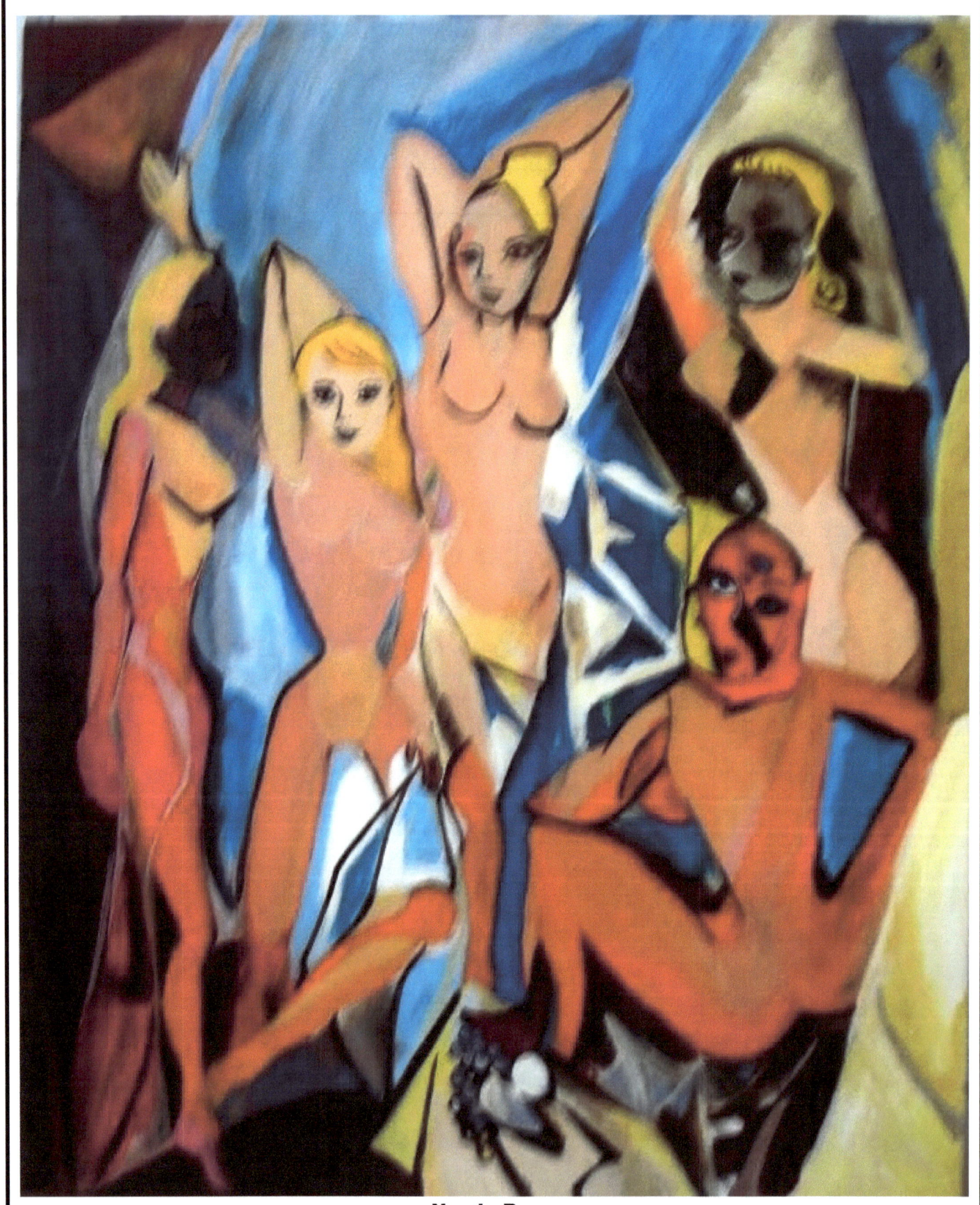

a Nowie Bowen

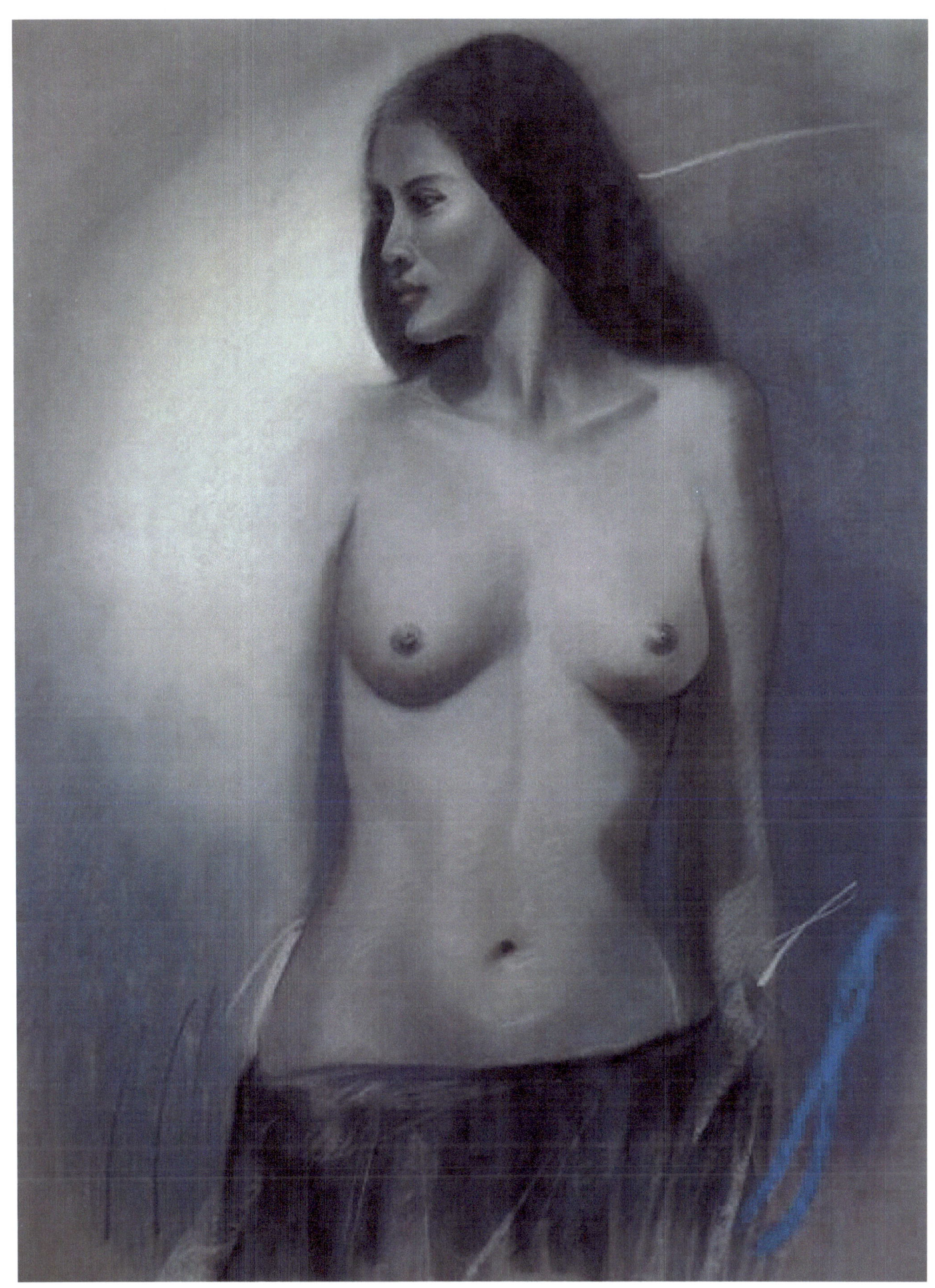

a Hermes Alegre

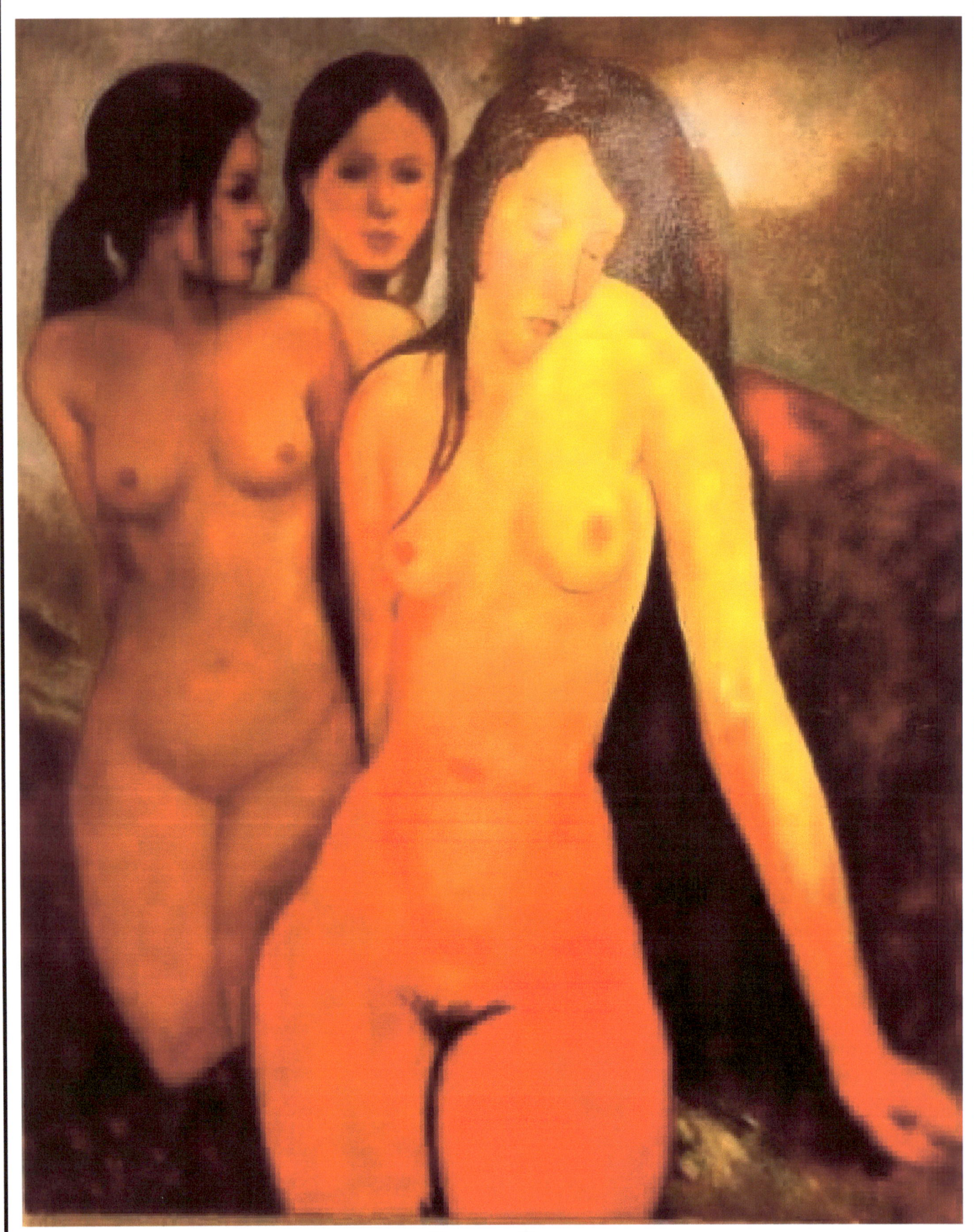

a Hermes Alegre

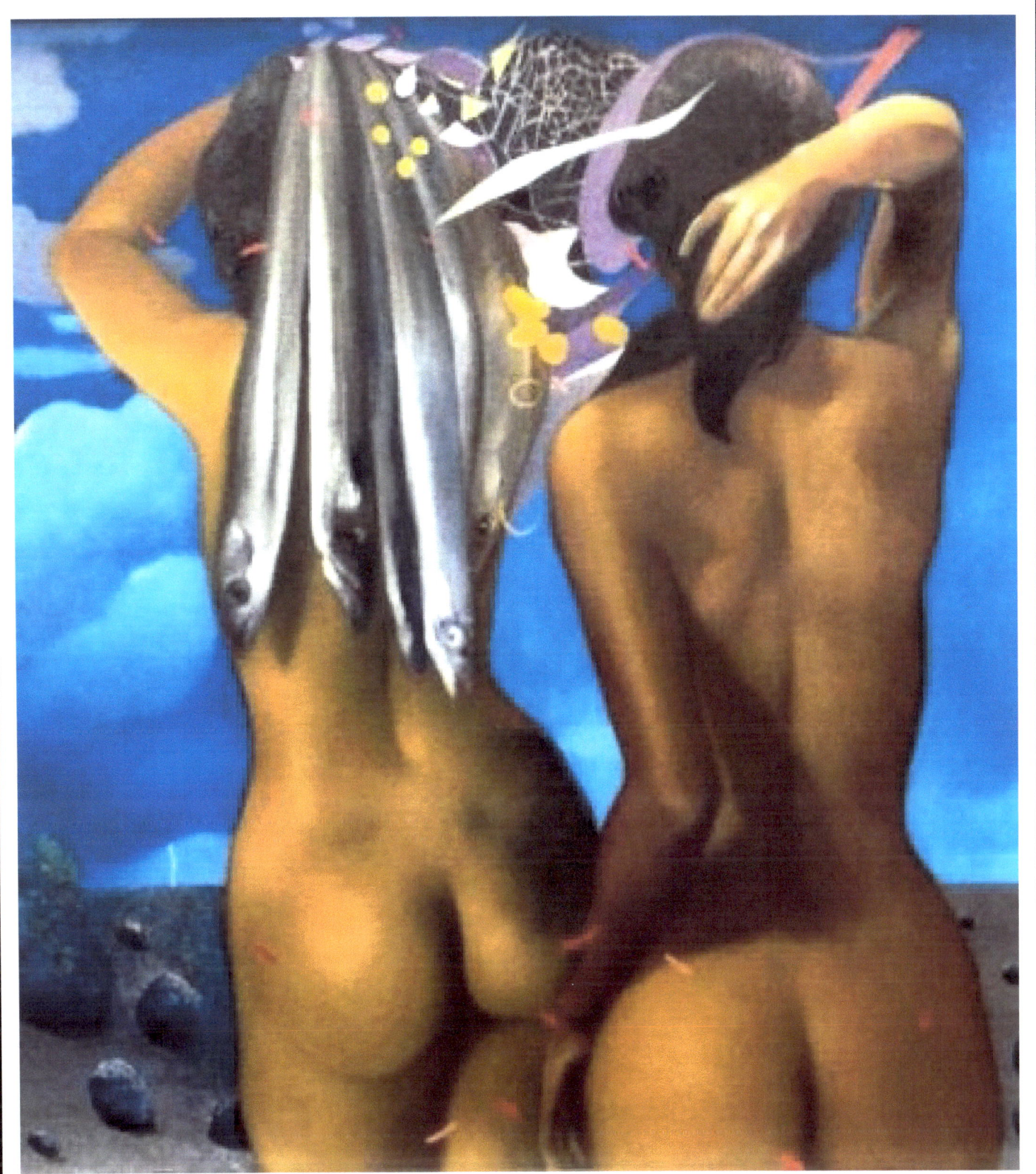

a Hermes Alegre

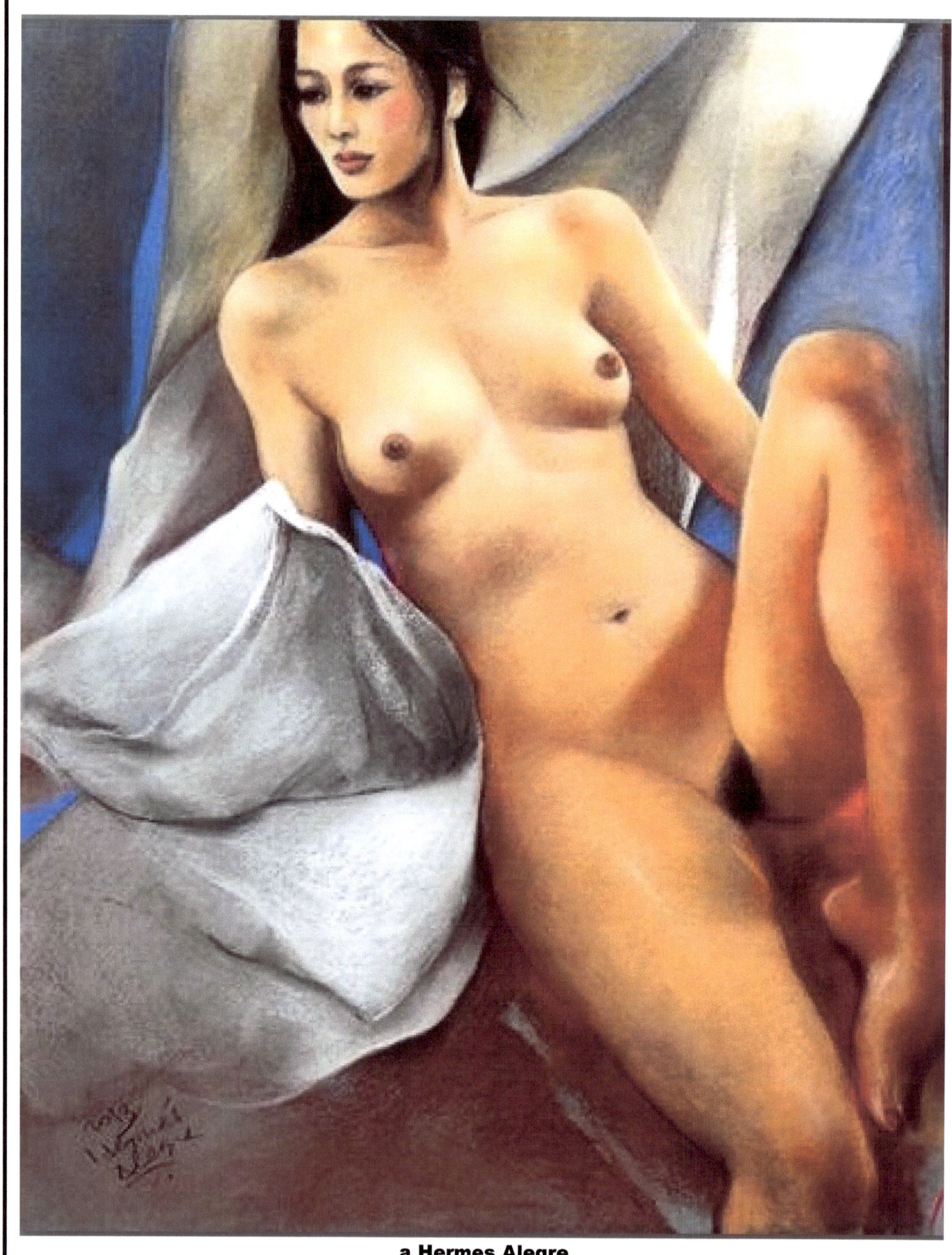

Fave Art - 11
a Hermes Alegre

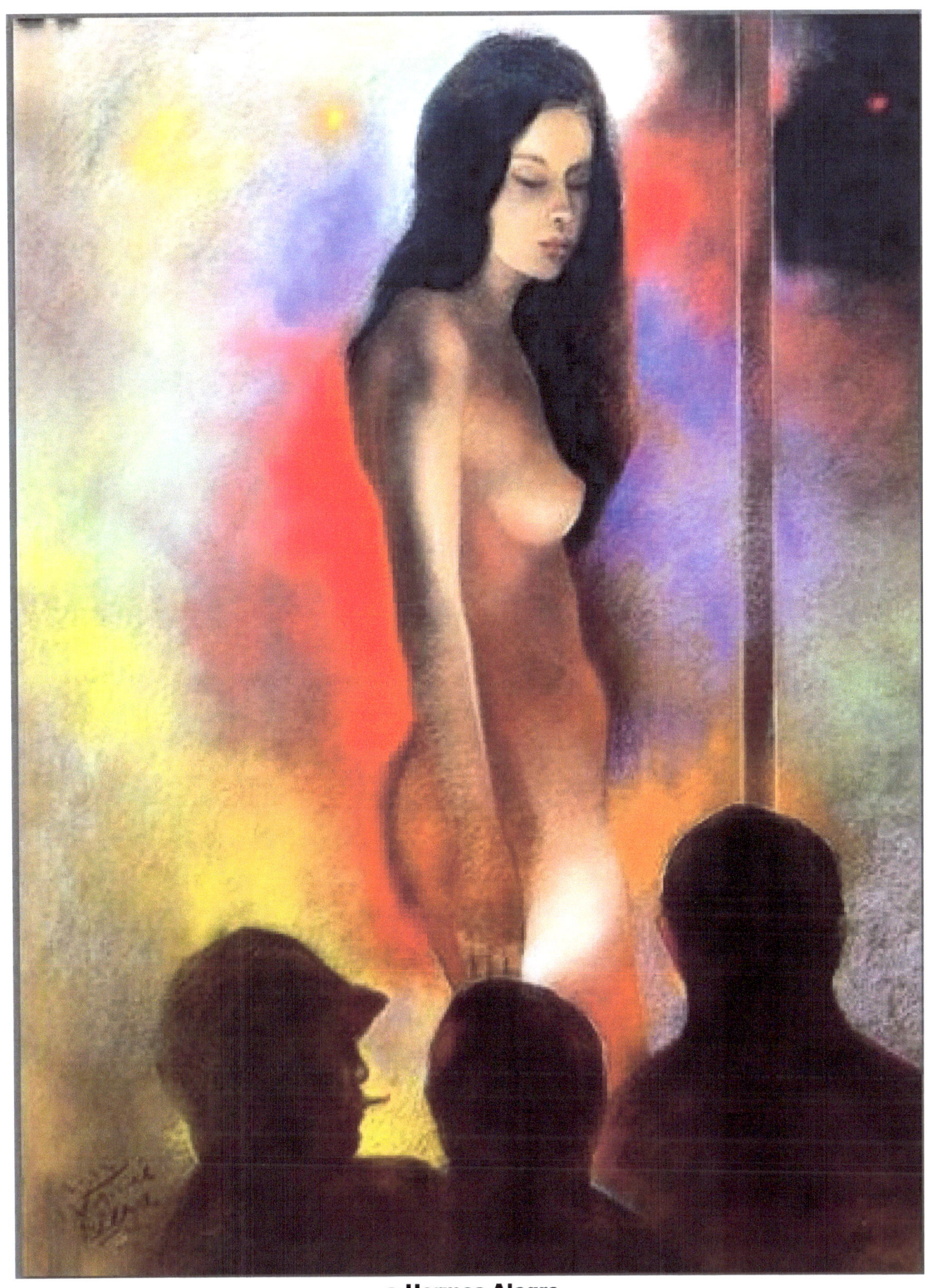

a Hermes Alegre

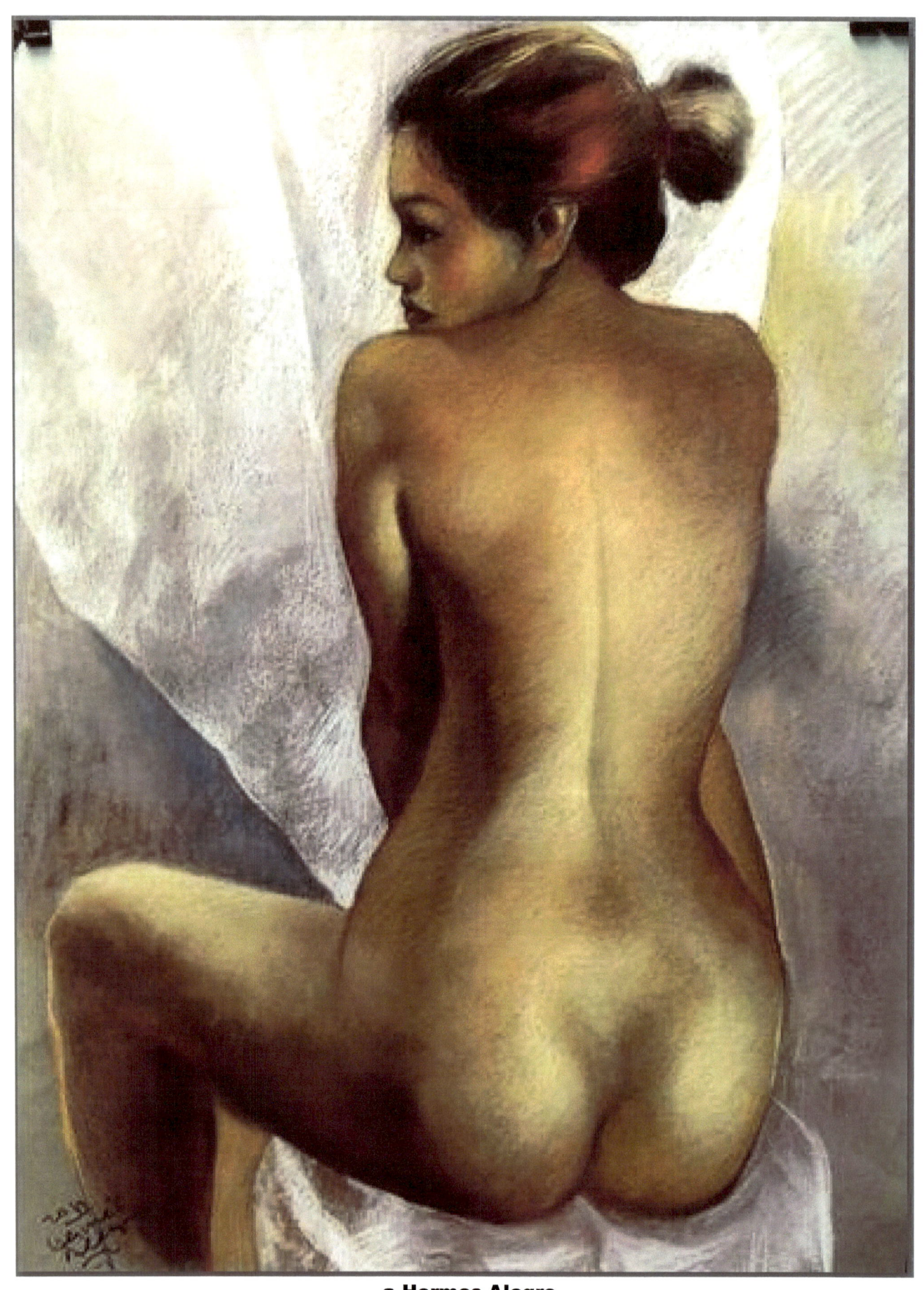

a Hermes Alegre

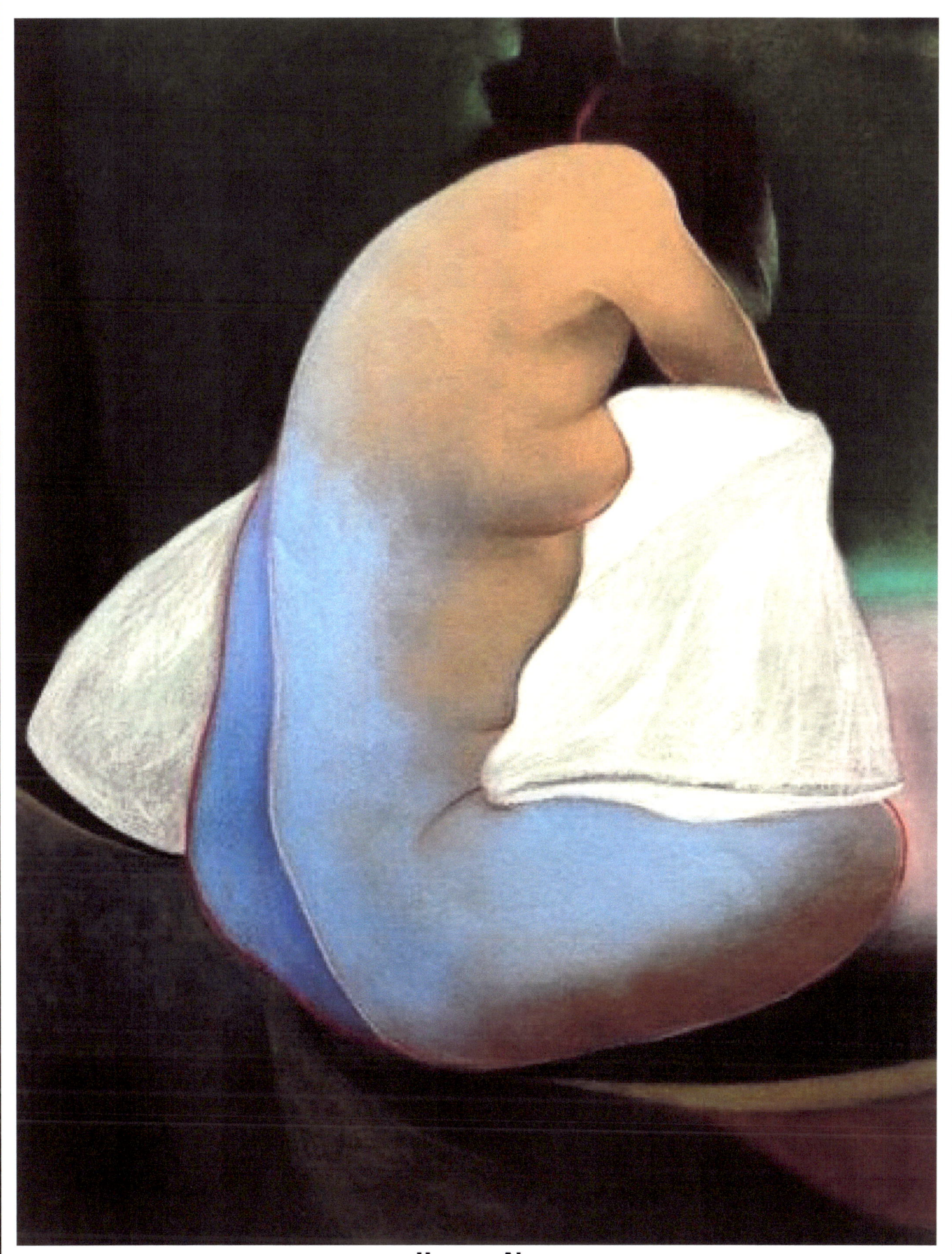

a Hermes Alegre

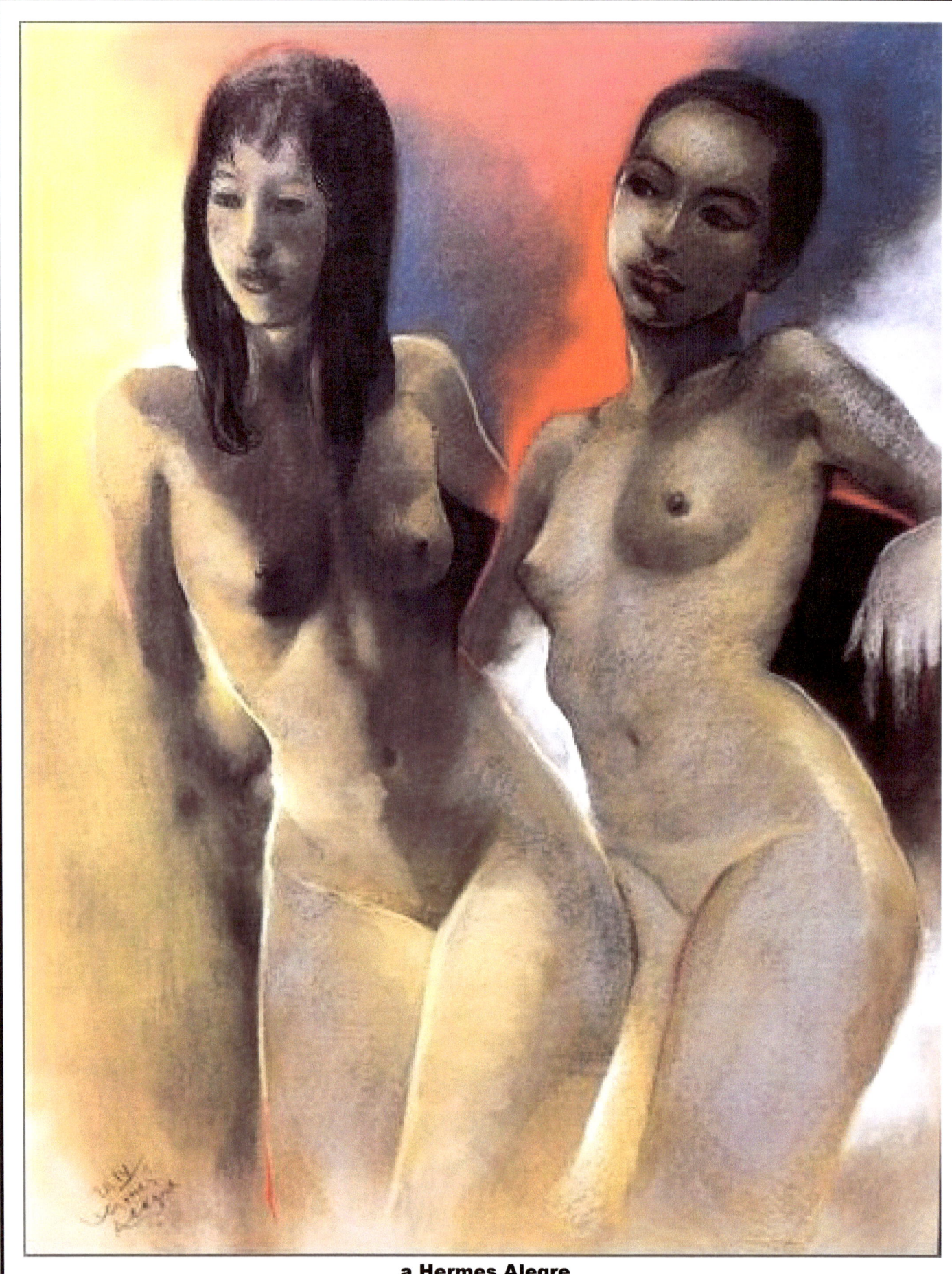

a Hermes Alegre

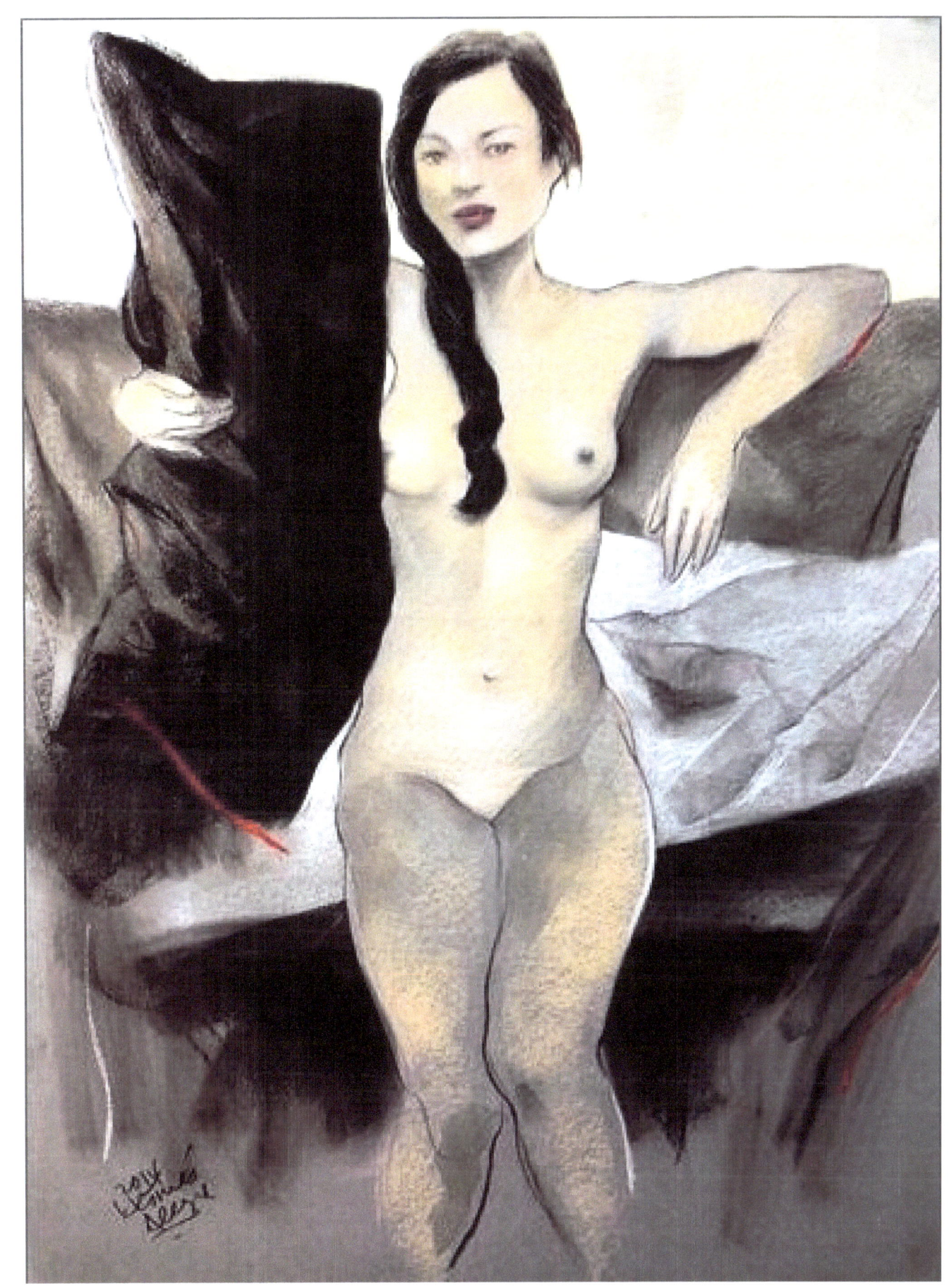

a Hermes Alegre

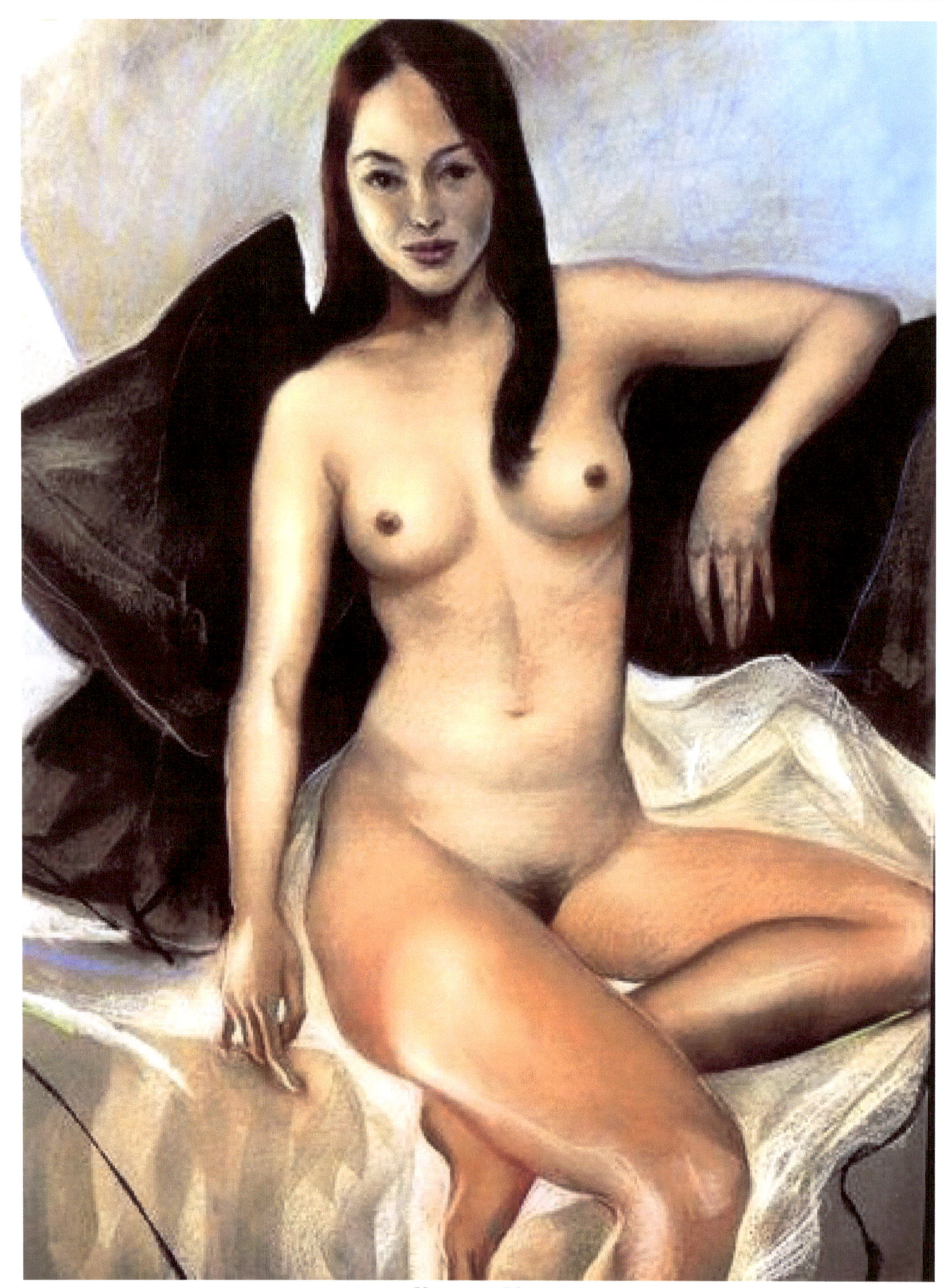

a Hermes Alegre

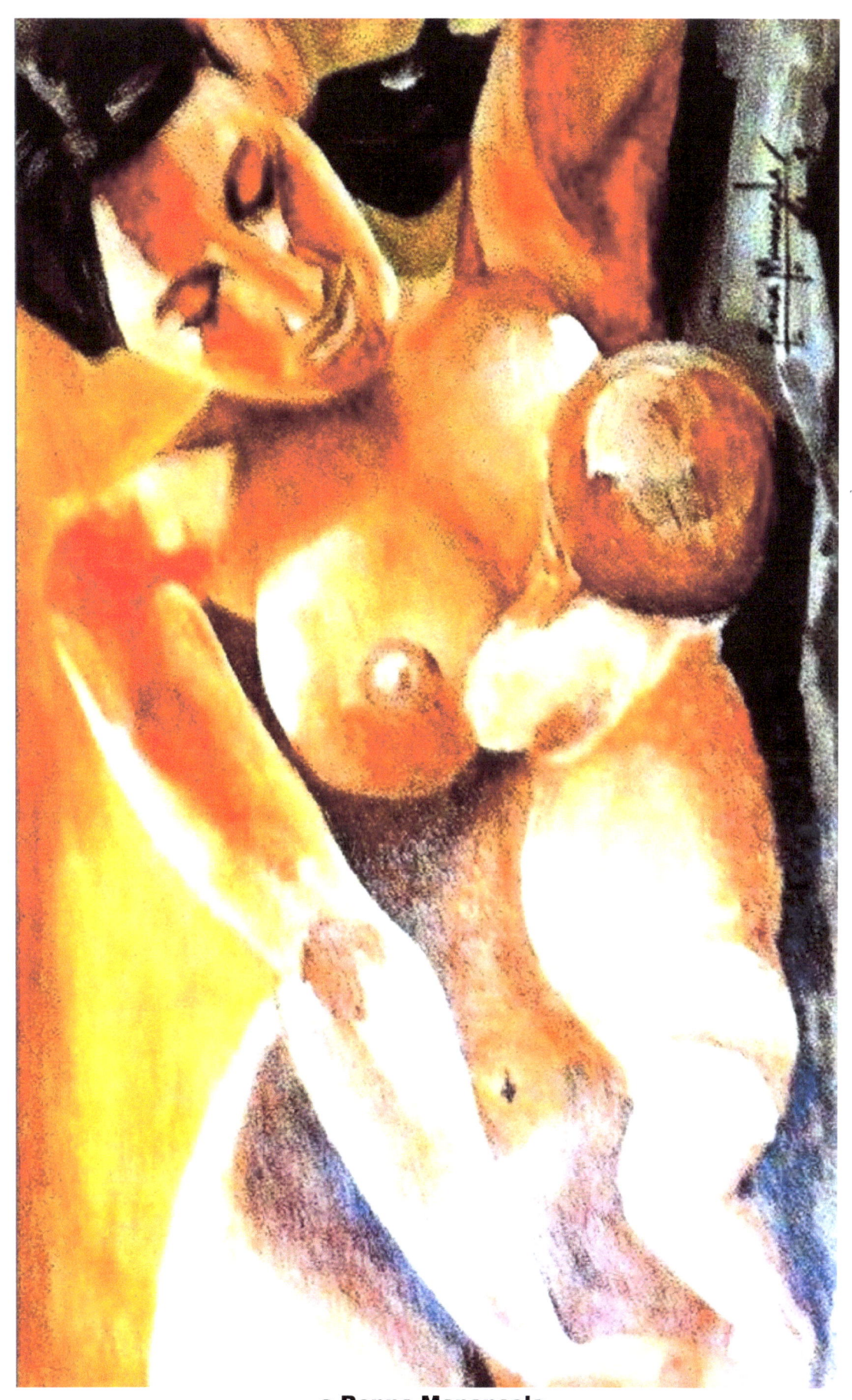

a Ronna Manansala

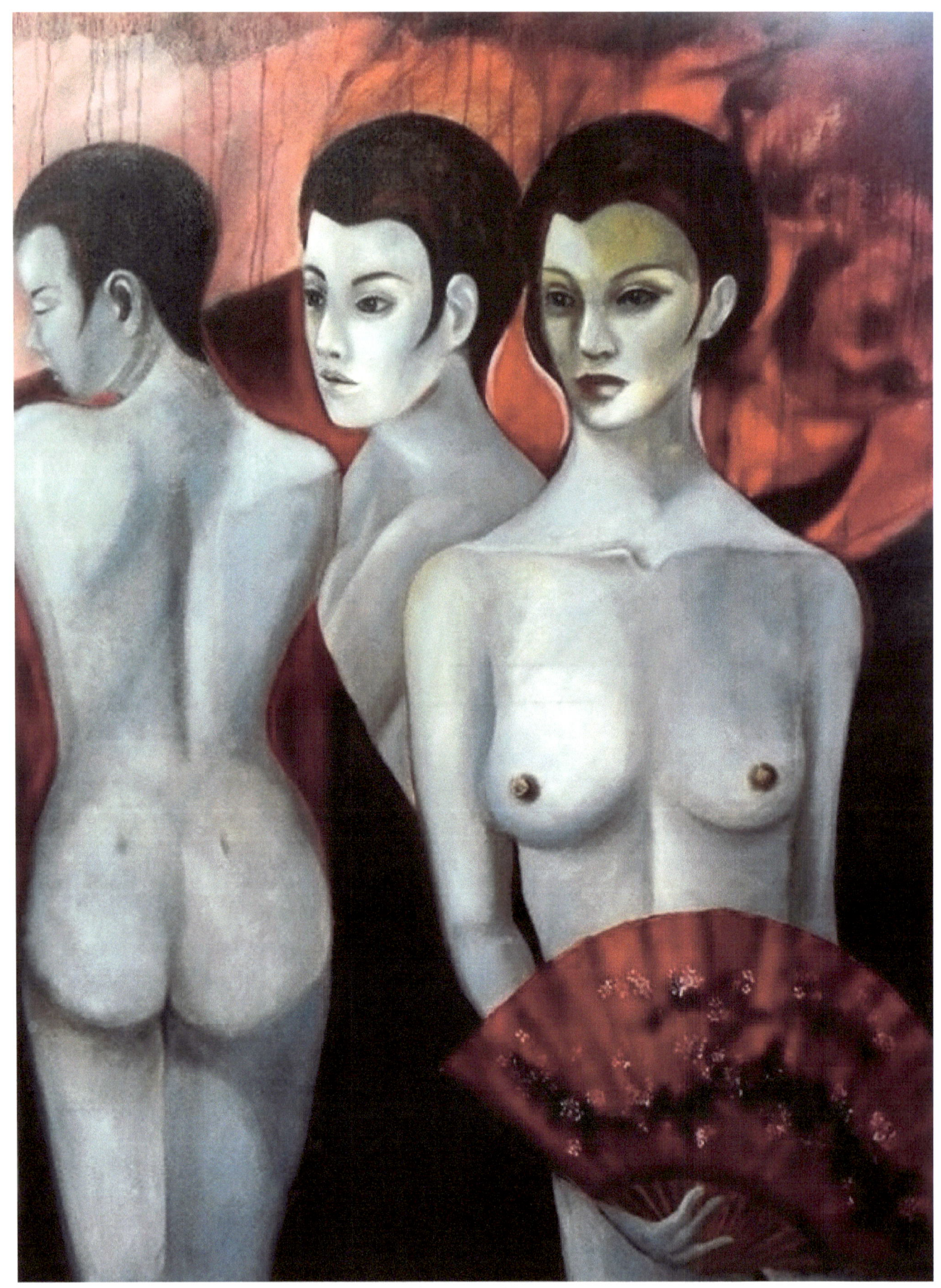

a Hermes Alegre

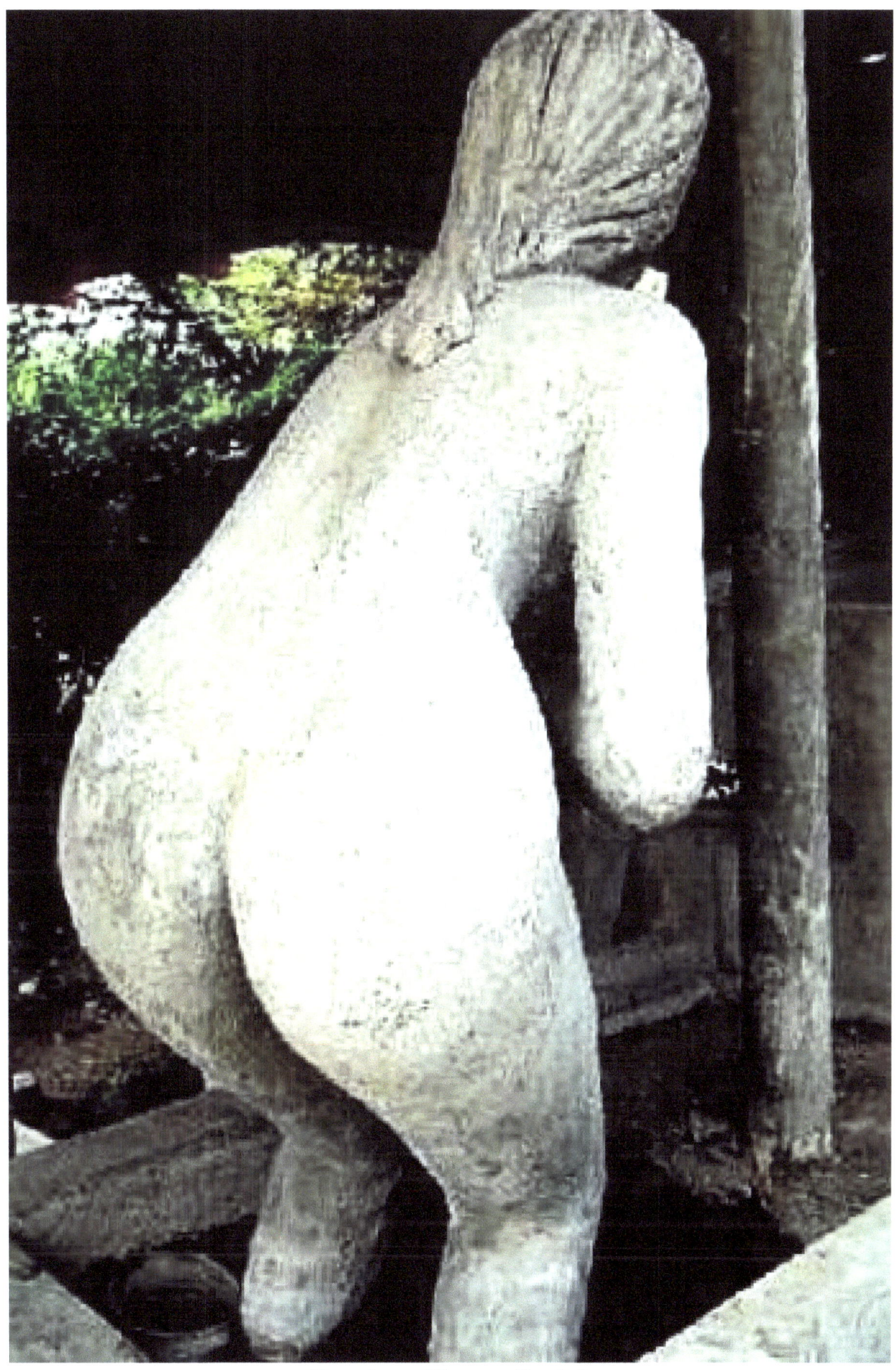

a Napoleon Abueva Sculpture

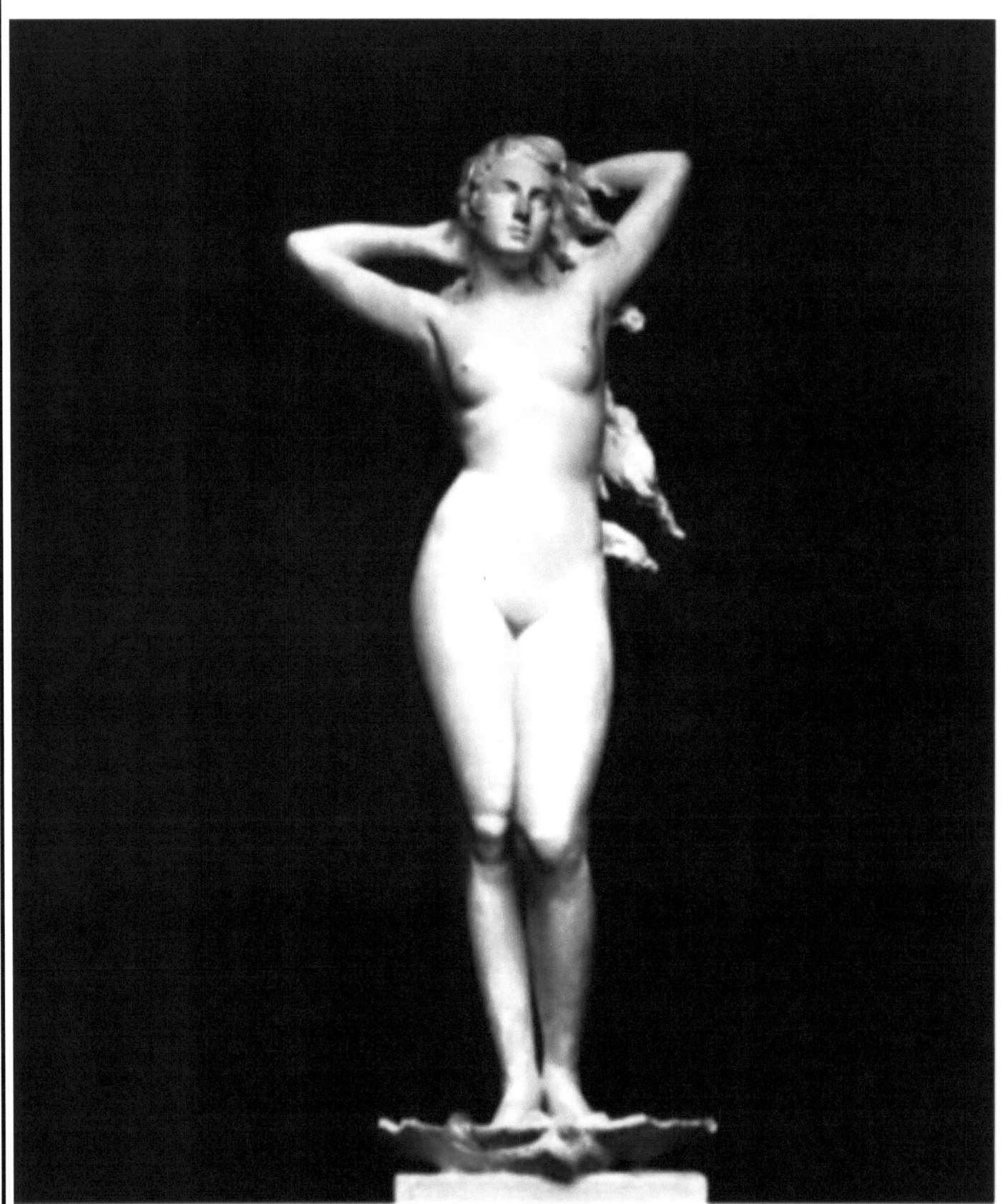

By famous Sculptor and Artist Tolentino, this Venus used to be displayed at Phil. National Museum, but now disappeared. (image by Clara de la Groce, Courtesy of Phils My Phils at facebook)